AALIYAH

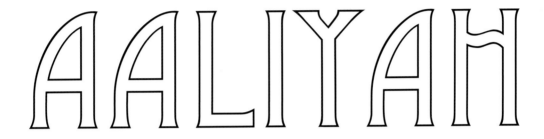

TIM FOOTMAN

PLEXUS, LONDON

All rights reserved including the right of
reproduction in whole or in part in any form
Copyright © 2003 by Plexus Publishing Ltd
Published by Plexus Publishing Limited
55a Clapham Common Southside
London SW4 9BX
Tel: 020 7622 2440
Fax: 020 7622 2441
www.plexusbooks.com
First printing 2003

British Library Cataloguing in Publication Data

Footman, Tim
    Aaliyah
    1.Aaliyah 2.Singers - United States - Biography 3.Soul
    musicians - United States - Biography
    I.Title
    782.4'21644'092

    ISBN 0 85965 327 7

Printed by Bookprint, Barcelona
Cover design by Phil Gambrill
Book design by Jay Parker

CONTENTS

INTRODUCTION

'No scale can measure secret treasures.'

IT'S ONLY AFTERWARDS that you notice the significance . . . Doom-laden church bells toll in the distance. A female voice cackles like a wicked witch, the aural personification of evil and damnation. 'Aaliyah,' she intones. 'Wake up . . . You just now entered into the next level . . .'

You can read too much into some things. 'Beats 4 da Streets', the first track on Aaliyah's second album, *One in a Million*, was originally conceived as nothing more than a campy but spooky intro. But when, five years later, the singer died in shocking circumstances, it seemed like some kind of premonition. If Aaliyah truly had 'entered into the next level', then that term didn't only apply in hindsight to religious belief in an afterlife (although God was always at the top of her acknowledgements list), but to the select list of iconic superstars who died before their time. Many, like Aaliyah, perished in tragic accidents – Buddy Holly, Otis Redding, James Dean, and, representing a different branch of showbusiness and celebrity, Princess Diana – while for others – Kurt Cobain, Tupac Shakur, Marilyn Monroe, River Phoenix – the dark forces of drugs, depression and violence were at work.

'I wanna sing, I wanna dance, I wanna act. I wanna be the best at what I do. That's about it.'

One effect of such an untimely death is that it becomes very difficult to view an artist objectively. There's always an overriding feeling of, as one of Aaliyah's last recordings asks, 'What

If?' The young Aaliyah had ambitions to become another Barbra Streisand or Whitney Houston, crossing over between the music business and the movie industry as a traditional 'all-round entertainer'. She was certainly on her way, with two well-received movie performances adding to the sense of wasted promise. However, her later recordings, and rumours of plans to collaborate with left-field titans Beck and Trent Reznor, hint at aspirations well beyond the MoR style of her girlhood idols. Her desire to imbue urban soul/R&B with new sonic possibilities makes her loss doubly poignant. We don't only mourn for the superstar she was about to become, but for further musical innovations that never came to pass.

'I stuck with my family and my deep belief in God.'

In Aaliyah's case, such speculation becomes ever more intense because she made herself into a figure of mystery. Even now, her fans debate such basic facts as her marital status. Who was this child prodigy, who pleased fans of commercial pop music while introducing them to new musical directions? What was the special quality that attracted such big R&B and hip-hop players as R. Kelly, Missy Elliott, Timbaland and Rodney Jerkins to her? What was the truth behind the hype, the mystique and the rumours?

She seemed to enjoy teasing outsiders about who 'the real Aaliyah' was. As she said of her performing persona, in the year she died, 'you get so used to it that it becomes second nature – the way you kind of turn on "you". Sometimes I'm not even aware of what I'm doing. It's not all for show, and it's not all put on. But at the same time, there are things that I keep for myself.' Even those close to her seemed unable to penetrate her mystique, particularly in the early days: 'my parents would tell me so many times: "We don't really know what you're thinking, what's going on with you? We don't get you at all."'

Since her death, everything now seems laced with eerie significance. Her last movie role was as a vampire – a creature that triumphs over death itself. Even a recurrent dream she spoke of now reads like a grim portent: 'It's dark in my favourite dream,' she told the German magazine *Die Zeitof*, shortly before she died. 'Someone is following me, I'm scared. Then suddenly I lift off, far away. How do I feel? As if I'm swimming in air, weightless. Nobody can touch me.'

Aaliyah exercised her talent in a musical genre – commercial, hip-hop-influenced R&B – that's often criticised for a prepon-

'I've always known what I wanted and I go after it no matter what.'

derance of hype and image, even more so than other modern musical styles. Many performers, signed up for their looks or their attitude rather than their talent, are left to flounder when the next batch of new flesh comes along. There are a hell of a lot of people more concerned with sipping expensive cocktails, or flashing ostentatious jewellery, than creating music that's anything more than a yell 'to all my homies in the house'.

But Aaliyah was different. Her talent had been evident since she was a small child, and, even in her twenties, she displayed the same childlike delight in performing. It was this uncomplicated, unaffected charm that distinguished her from the prima

Aaliyah stares down the camera during a Vibe *photo shoot, February 1998.*

donnas and egomaniac *faux*-gangstas who demand exactly the right vintage champagne in their jacuzzi. She was a home girl in the best sense of the term, deeply loyal to the family who supported her thoughout her career, only to walk behind her, dazed with grief, on her final journey.

'I don't know what's going to happen in the next five or ten years. At some point I wanted to have a family and settle down, but I don't see that happening for a long time because I really love this. This is my life, my world.'

There were certainly a few downturns in Aaliyah's life, both personally and professionally. She had only just settled into a happy emotional relationship shortly before she died. And, in a bitter irony, none of her records ever topped the charts until she was no longer around to soak up the adulation. Maybe Aaliyah's belated success was due to a knee-jerk sympathetic reaction. For the circumstances of her death will always loom disproportionately large, whenever people think of her. But it's her life, not her tragic end, that we're here to celebrate.

Any number of books could be written on the 'What If?' element of Aaliyah's short, shining career. But this book focuses on the facts, the 22 brief years that make up the life of a performer who was truly 'One in a Million'.

Let's all enter into the next level.

*Aaliyah captivated the camera with her sensuality and mystique. (*Vibe *magazine, February 1998)*

1: SEARCHING FOR STARDOM

'I still remember walking through the park . . .'

'Those Were The Days'

NEW YORK CITY, 1979. Brooklyn: the most populous of the city's five boroughs. 1979 doesn't seem so long ago, but in many ways it was a different planet. Imagine it: no CDs; no MTV; no PlayStations. Michael Jackson was still black, but most mainstream music broadcasting was still whiter than white. The big noise in the clubs during the past decade had been disco – but disco was dying on its gold lamé ass, hijacked by the Bee Gees and John Travolta for the movie *Saturday Night Fever*.

In its place was a new sound, New York's own sound. It was a fusion of Jamaican sound systems and the wit and wisdom of the Bronx. Add some graffiti from a spraycan, twirl on your head, and, as the

'My parents just tell me, "If you know what you want you should stay determined and go for it." You can do anything.'

Sugarhill Gang put it, you've got 'the rhythm of the boogie, the beat.'

To many outsiders, it sounded like gibberish, but it was following in a great tradition of African-American music. Rock 'n' roller Little Richard, in the Fifties, had hollered out, 'Awopbopaloobopawopbamboom!' Soul man Otis Redding, in the Sixties, had sung 'Fa-Fa-Fa-Fa-Fa'. The latest addition to the lexicon of popular culture was, of course, called hip-hop.

Diane and Michael Haughton were residents of the Bedford-Stuyvesant area of Brooklyn. It was the biggest black neighbourhood in the whole of New York City, later

Third Annual Aid Fundraiser at the Sam Goody Store in Los Angeles, 1994.

the location for Spike Lee's incendiary movie *Do the Right Thing*. The Haughtons were a musical family, especially Diane, who had a beautiful voice. Before becoming a full-time mother she had sung professionally in musicals touring the country, and her singing continued to be a feature of the Haughtons' close-knit family life. But, on 16 January 1979, it's unlikely that their minds were on the new musical revolution brewing in their hometown. It was the day Diane gave birth to their second child, christened Aaliyah Dana – the first name being an Arabic word for 'the highest' or 'the most exalted'. It's the feminine version of the surname taken by the young boxer originally called Cassius Clay, when he converted to Islam and became Muhammad Ali. In black America, the bearer of such a name had much to live up to. Aaliyah came to love her name. 'It's a beautiful name, I'm very proud of it', she later said. And she did her best to live up to it, as she famously later declared, 'I try every day.'

The Haughtons also had family history in another city crucial to the development of African-American music: Detroit, Michigan. When Aaliyah was just four years old, the family of four (including her devoted elder brother, Rashad) moved out of Brooklyn and headed back west to their relatives' hometown. Diane's brother Barry Hankerson lived there with his wife, and their son Jomo, so the two families quickly formed a clan; Aaliyah and Rashad spending a lot of time with their cousin. Speaking to the writer Christopher John Farley in 2001, Jomo reminisced about their day to day life. 'Growing up we lived five blocks apart. I used to walk them home from school sometimes when Aunt Diane couldn't get there and stuff.'

Detroit is not a picturesque city, but it's famous for two

'It was always part of my thing that I want people to look at me as an entertainer.'

products. Both were constructed on an assembly line, and both helped to define the identity of the USA in the 20th century: the cars built by Ford Motors, and the glorious, life-affirming music of the Tamla Motown label. Motown, home to soul legends including Diana Ross, Marvin Gaye and Stevie Wonder, in the sixties and seventies, gave Detroit a powerful identity. It has retained its position as a centre for popular music made by black artists, borne of hard graft and infused with pride in its cultural origin. In the eighties the tradition was continued by the dance music of innovators such as Juan Atkins, Derrick May and Kevin Saunderson. And in the nineties, one of Detroit's most famous exports, although white, gave the world his own attitude-infused take on the city and its music. The real Slim Shady, aka Eminem, has helped immortalise Detroit further, and his feature film debut *8Mile* has bought Detroit alive for a new world-wide audience, portraying a gritty urban landscape, filled with residents whose dreams flourish amidst decay and disaffection.

Aaliyah's artistic development would be shaped by the move to Detroit. She spent her childhood in a city steeped in music and industry. Her ambition, determination, and work ethic, borne out of her own drive and nurtured by her family, was also influenced by her environment. Aaliyah might have lived in a nice middle class neighbourhood, but all the walls of Detroit breathe a musical history, one that continues to this day, and now encloses Aayliah in its legacy.

Whatever Aaliyah was going to do with her life, it was fairly certain she wasn't going to work on a production line at Ford's. For there was a family connection to the legendary music-making machine begun by Berry Gordy, Jr. at 2648 West Grand Boulevard. Diane Haughton's brother, Barry Hankerson, was married at that time to Gladys Knight, one of the company's star attractions in the late 1960s. And Gladys, in her turn, would later have a pivotal role in propelling Aaliyah to stardom.

But for now, little Miss Haughton was just another happy-go-lucky kid from a comfortable, if not wealthy, home on the west side of Motor City. The only thing that set her apart from her schoolfriends was the musical ability that was apparent almost as soon as she was walking and talking. Her mother was a talented singer, and little Aaliyah soon showed a similar gift, copying the music she heard around her. By the mid-Eighties, when Whitney Houston became a big name, Aaliyah was quickly able to match the soul diva note for note. Says Jomo, 'I remember that once Rashad and Aaliyah got to Detroit, that Aaliyah and Aunt Diane would always

Aaliyah the home-girl, in a shoot for Tommy Hilfiger, 1996.

be around the house singing. Growing up, Aaliyah would sing the whole Whitney Houston album and the whole Luther Vandross album around the house.' Diane and Michael had no qualms about supporting their daughter in her wish to become an entertainer and were more than instrumental in helping her develop her career. Aaliyah later explained, 'When I told my parents I wanted to embark along this path, they were with me all the way.' This loving closeness and support was something Aaliyah always derived strength from. She would later tell *Vibe* magazine, 'I'm a survivor, and I can handle anything. I'm very confident about that. I come from a very strong family and they are always there to protect me.'

'I was a pretty popular kid, but I think I was like all kids and went through an awkward stage.'

Aaliyah was lucky enough to attend Gesu Elementary School, which had a tradition of putting on large-scale musical shows. In her first grade she landed the role of an orphan in *Annie*, her first experience of a paying audience, and of the discipline required to entertain the public. It's tempting to see this as a defining moment, the point at which she became set on a showbusiness career. Aaliyah later described how she felt being on stage. Even though she had only one line to deliver, she loved every minute of it. 'That's when I told myself, I've got to do this forever.' And as she later reflected, 'I was very, very shy back then, but going out for the play helped me come out of my shell. I loved the camaraderie of it all. . .To be able to act and sing now is the fulfillment of all that I've wanted to do.' A similarly revelatory moment occured when Rashad took the young Aaliyah to the cinema to see a Barbra Streisand film. Later, she remembered gazing up at the screen, and thinking, 'One day I'll be up there like Barbra Streisand. Acting, singing, she does it all.'

Of course, it's never that straightforward. If Aaaliyah was going to make it in showbiz, she was going to need plenty of support and nurturing on her way to the top. When she was ten years old, her parents enrolled her with a singing coach named Wendelin Petty, who was able to hone Aaliyah's raw talents. Peddy remembers Aaliyah as not only talented but also focused: 'As a ten year old she knew exactly what she wanted to do. She knew she wanted to be an entertainer.' By this stage, she had already been entering talent shows and singing at local weddings for a couple of years. She exhibited no fear of big audiences, but seemed to thrive on the adrenalin they produced. It was time to demonstrate her talent on a bigger stage.

Star Search was an American TV institution, giving unknowns the chance to try their luck before a nationwide audience. For a few it was the first step to stardom. For many, it was a solitary flicker of public recognition before they faded back into obscurity. And there was always the thrilling possibility for the audience that some acts would be truly, tooth-achingly atrocious.

Of course, Aaliyah was too talented to fall into that category. Despite her tender years, her rendition of the Rodgers/Hart standard 'My Funny Valentine' (previously recorded by singing legends as diverse as Ella Fitzgerald and Elvis Costello) was no embarrassment. However, it wasn't the massive crowd-pleaser needed in the cut-throat atmosphere of a national talent contest, so her biggest exposure thus far also led to her biggest disappointment.

A fresh-faced young Aaliyah backstage at the Life Beat Urban Aid event, 1994.

'To be able to act and sing now is the fulfillment of all that I've wanted to do.'

Left: Aaliyah the fly girl, backstage before a New York gig in 1994. Above: Aaliyah performing at the Forum in 1997.

'My mother and father grew up with Sammy Davis, Jr. and Fred Astaire, and those people had to do it all.'

Young Aaliyah was at a crossroads. She could have taken the setback as a sign that she could make a few bucks serenading tipsy wedding guests, but that any chance of Whitney Houston-style megastardom would remain a dream. Or she could take it as an impetus to work harder, to hone her professionalism. When the judges' verdict had been announced, Aaliyah had cried. But years later, with hindsight, she was able to see that losing on *Star Search* had been an important experience: 'I learned about rejection that day. But I realised you have to dust yourself down and try again.'

It was time to take advantage of family connections. Gladys Knight was performing a season of cabaret dates in Las Vegas, and she was happy to give young Aaliyah a little exposure. While it's fair to say eleven-year-old Aaliyah wouldn't have joined her aunt on stage at Bally's Casino if not for her uncle, Barry Hankerson, it's equally true that, if she hadn't had the talent to justify Ms Knight's faith in her, she'd have been on a plane back to Detroit after the first bum note.

Gladys Knight knew better than anyone that it required a combination of talent, persistence and luck to stay in the music business. Like Aaliyah, she began her professional career at an early age, winning *The Ted*

'Having a strong family base and a belief in God enables me to weather the storms.'

Mack Amateur Hour when she was just seven years old. She was performing with her backing group, the Pips, during the heady days of the 1950s, when earthy R&B was giving way to the more sophisticated sound that came to be known as soul music. In the 1960s, she was signed to Detroit's own Motown label, but lacked the glamorous image of Diana Ross and the Supremes or the dynamic charisma of the Temptations. With the Pips, she recorded the original version of 'I Heard It Through the Grapevine', only to see Marvin Gaye's version of the song become a number one smash on both sides of the Atlantic. It wasn't until she left Motown for Buddah Records in the mid-Seventies that she was able to live up to her early promise, cutting the classic 'Midnight Train to Georgia'.

Gladys Knight kept a high profile well into the Eighties, recording the AIDS benefit single 'That's What Friends Are For' with Dionne Warwick, Stevie Wonder and Elton John, and the James Bond theme 'Licence to Kill'. Never a soul icon on the level of Aretha Franklin or James Brown, she still maintained the respect of her peers, and the loyalty of older fans who appreciated well-crafted, sentimental songs delivered with style and professionalism. She also avoided the personal problems that had plagued many of her fellow soul performers, such as Marvin Gaye.

So it was a discerning audience that met young Aaliyah at the casino. Gladys Knight was guaranteed to turn in a note-perfect, totally committed performance, which anyone who shared the stage with her would at least have to equal. 'I was able to learn a lot from that,' Aaliyah said of the experience. "I began to work the stage and get the audience into it. I also learned to have fun out there." For Gladys, it was also a learning experience, as she felt the full force of Aaliyah's talent: 'When she first performed with me in Las Vegas, she was still quite young, but she already had it – that spark the world would later see and fall in love with.'

Aaliyah's performance was a triumph, and restored any self-confidence that may have

Left: Aaliyah, accessorising with her trademark sunglasses, at the Life Beat Urban Aid event, 1995.

been eroded by *Star Search*. Whatever that indefinable 'It Factor' might be – charisma, star quality, call it what you will – it was clear that she had it. As *Star Search* judge Ed McMahon put it, 'There's a thing you see when somebody walks on stage. I call it "the fire". They got that inner fire, which has nothing to do with the schooling, nothing to do

'You know we're in a business where things are unpredictable.'

with the teacher, nothing to do with the parents.' Gladys Knight echoed this sentiment with the words, 'I knew she had enormous talents and an intrinsic gift.'

But, despite her talents, Aaliyah still was a sensible girl, grounded in reality. She knew that, even if she did hit the big time, stardom might not be a long-term proposition. The showbiz files are full of stars who dominated the world for a few months, then suddenly found that nobody was returning their calls. (Does anyone remember MC Hammer, or Milli Vanilli?) If Aaliyah was going to wake up one morning and find she was just anonymous Ms A. D. Haughton once more, she needed to know she had the skills and qualifications to make it in the real world. And even after she did hit the big time, and the idea of longevity became a reality, Aaliyah still applied this principle in her working life, stating, 'Sometimes people negate the fact that training is important . . . I still take vocal lessons. I take dance . . . I take acting lessons.'

Luckily for her, she found a way to simultaneously pursue her academic studies while developing her skills as a performer. The Detroit High School for the Fine and Performing Arts was founded in the early Nineties, modelled on the world-famous New York School of Performing Arts immortalised in the movie and TV show *Fame*. The Detroit school provided a balance between rigorous academic instruction and a grounding in the skills necessary to make it in the entertainment business.

Aaliyah's ambitions didn't stop at making it as a singer, either. Her idols were performers like Whitney Houston and Barbra Streisand, who worked in at least one other field. As she later explained, when she was growing up the 'all-round entertainer' was her role model. 'I've been taking acting lessons since I was very young,' she said, 'I still do to this day. My mother and father grew up with Sammy Davis, Jr. and Fred Astaire, and those people had to do it all. This is how I was raised; this is how I was trained. It was always part of my thing that I want people to look at me as an entertainer.'

Her music would be in a different style from that of her heroines, but that was just an accident of timing and fashion. The jazz-influenced showtunes of Streisand and

'I go through the same problems all young people go through.'

the mainstream soul ballads that defined Houston's career were of their time, in much the same way that R&B and hip-hop were of the mid-Nineties.

Complementing her vocal and acting ability, Aaliyah's main subject at the Detroit School was to be dance. For she didn't just have Grammys and gold discs in her sights – she dreamt of Tonys, Emmys, Oscars, a star on the Hollywood Walk of Fame, and handprints outside Graumann's Chinese Theater. As she later joked to *i-D* magazine, quoting the immortal opening lines from *Fame*, 'You pay in sweat and right here's where you start paying.'

By the time Aaliyah graduated in 1997 – proficient in maths, history and science, as well as dance, music and acting – she had already completed two albums. Her uncle, Barry

Hankerson, had set up a record company called Blackground who were distributed by Jive Records, a label with a healthy roster of R&B, hip-hop and soul talent. Hankerson's first signing to Blackground was his own niece. The label was very much a family affair with Aaliyah's cousin Jomo, Hankerson's son, also joining the roster of staff (he would eventually become president after seven years). Meanwhile Aaliyah's brother Rashad, took on the job of being her creative consultant, a role he had always fulfilled naturally as her big brother. Said Aaliyah, 'he's always been there for me. So I just started introducing him to people as my creative consultant. Eventually the title just stuck.'

'What is the real me? It's hard to say . . . I have a feeling for the hard-core street life, but I like to hang out in malls.'

One of the label's biggest hitters was a performer, writer and producer by the name of Robert S. Kelly, known to his fans simply as R. Kelly. Born on the South Side of Chicago in 1967, one of four children brought up by a single mother, Kelly was seen my many as a natural successor to the legendary Marvin Gaye for his ability to combine the twin obsessions of soul music – religion and raw, panting sex. By 1993, he was one of the most talked-about new stars in the entertainment industry, largely on account of his raunchy album *12 Play*. Although Kelly wasn't a hellraiser or a bad boy, he was happy to admit that he had an eye for the ladies – and, if the rumours were to be believed, he was particularly fond of younger ladies. This inclination has been a major inspiration for his songwriting. Kelly loves to love, and it shines through in all his work. In fact he has stated that he channels his desires into his music: 'You see a woman who just drives you wild, and not having her can make you wanna cry out, sing out.'

It was Hankerson who had the idea of putting his sweet young niece, only just into her early teens, in a studio with R&B's latest love god. Many men would have been wary about even allowing such a meeting. But, whatever misgivings hindsight may bring, the fruits of an encounter between Ms Aaliyah Dana Haughton and Mr Robert S. Kelly were guaranteed not to be dull.

2: STREET THING

'Her voice was distinctive, off the top, when you heard it
on the radio, you knew who it was. There ain't many
artists out there that have their own identity.'

Jermaine Dupri

R&B, OR RHYTHM AND BLUES, is one of the most confusingly diverse musical styles, straddling three different eras. The original R&B sprang out of jive music and jazz in the Forties, almost exclusively a black American school of performance. As its name suggests, it added a rhythm section (drums and double bass, later bass guitar) to the structures of the blues chants that developed from African-American slave songs. R&B was at its most popular in the early-to-mid-1950s, although at the time it was practically unknown to white audiences. The most important performers included Ray Charles, Etta James, Lloyd Price, and Ruth Brown. Gradually, it was edged out by the multi-racial sounds of rock 'n' roll and, a few years later, gave birth to a smoother style of music that became known as soul.

In the early Sixties, a crop of British musicians like the Rolling Stones and John Mayall's Blues Breakers (featuring a young Eric Clapton) combined the

'The image is a part of me. I wear the baggy pants, the hats, the whole nine.'

style of original R&B with that of Chicago blues performers. But the most recent form of R&B –the one that encompasses the music of Aaliyah – is the hip-hop-influenced strain of commercial soul music that came to prominence in the late Eighties. Encompassing a range of variations, such as new jack swing, it also came under the rather meaningless heading of 'urban contemporary' – a euphemism for 'mainly listened to by black people'. It's very much a producer-driven style, its big hitters including Teddy Riley and two important part-

nerships, Jimmy Jam and Terry Lewis and L. A. Reid and Babyface.

By the end of the 1990s, the new R&B had edged most other musical forms out of the American pop singles charts, and was making massive inroads into overseas territories. Although many of the performers – including Mary J. Blige, Jodeci, and Usher – had their roots in live gospel music, it was very much a studio-based form, relying on complex, multi-tracked vocals, and programmed rhythms and percussion. At first it was ignored by the mainstream music press, which preferred guitar-based rock and hip-hop. By the new millennium, however, the most commercial of the new R&B performers, such as the phenomenally successful Destiny's Child, were showing up on the covers of *Rolling Stone* and *NME*.

'I make time for being a kid but I also know when to put on my business hat.'

When Aaliyah's debut album, *Age Ain't Nothing but a Number*, hit the stores in 1994, it went under her name. There's a strong argument, however, for crediting the album to R. Kelly: after all, he produced it, mixed it, and wrote all bar one of the songs, while Aaliyah's contribution was to give voice to Kelly's lyrics.

Ultimately the two complemented one another. While the words may have been all his, the delivery was all hers. And at this stage Aaliyah had no problem with Kelly taking the lead in the studio, saying, 'I don't mind being called his protégé because that's what I am.'

The cover photographs illustrate Aaliyah's role as Kelly's protegée. She poses against a concrete wall, looking slightly uncomfortable in her black and white 'fly girl' clothes, her beautiful eyes shaded by black sunglasses. Meanwhile, Kelly hovers in the background, moody, out of focus, his ear glued to a cellphone, keeping watch over his oh-so-young collaborator. For a young performer who had her heart set on emulating middle-of-the-road entertainers like Barbra Streisand, the switch to contemporary street culture was no easy transition. She carried it off with aplomb though, her natural beauty and poise lending her grace. And audience reaction to her image was extremely positive. Her look naturally appealed to male fans, but was also friendly enough not to alienate the female audience. R. Kelly fashioned her in his own image, and Aaliyah took her first step along the road to style icon status. And her presence was noted not just by the public but by fashion professionals. Hip hop designer Tommy Hilfiger, who Aaliyah went on to model for, later enthused, 'She made the hip hop look – women wearing men's clothes – sexy.'

There's a long tradition of young performers having their careers shaped by older producers. The legendary Phil Spector had several girl groups under his control, none of them (including his ex-wife Ronnie Spector, formerly of the Ronettes) achieving much success when they stopped working with him. More recently, producer-entrepreneurs such as Pete Waterman have taken any number of acts to number one, only to leave them behind when the novelty wore off.

Sometimes the tables are turned, of course. Stars such as Michael Jackson went on to even bigger things after breaking away from the image moulders of Motown. And Tina Turner's career reached new heights once she was free from her abusive control-freak husband, Ike.

Even without the benefit of hindsight, it's clear that Aaliyah could only fully show her potential once she gained some degree of control over her own career. For *Age Ain't Nothing*

Aaliyah, dressed down to impress, March 1995.

but a Number is not only an R. Kelly album in all but name, it's a pretty lame one at that. There are no truly classic songs, some of the arrangements are jaded and unimaginative, and the best ingredient, by far, is Aaliyah's voice. After all this was a girl who had been honing her sound, and finding her voice, from a very young age. As her singing teacher Peddy explained, 'She and her parents wanted her voice to be developed and they wanted her style to develop, so that when she sang she wouldn't seem like a copycat – what you'd hear would be all Aaliyah . . . She had such a great voice aged 10. Really a voice that some adults might wish they had.' Now Kelly was taking the opportunity to harness Aaliyah's talent, and the world would have its first taste of it.

> *'I really think it's kinda funny how people like to make things up about you just because they can't figure you out.'*

A brief intro seems to sum up the intended scope of the album, beginning with some gospel-style harmonies before crashing into the live sounds of a hip-hop concert. The gospel element is classy, while the hip-hop is run-of-the-mill. It's emblematic of the album. When Aaliyah sticks to her soul and gospel roots, she's unbeatable. But Kelly's attempt to inject some urban credibility into the sound is at best unconvincing, at worst downright embarrassing.

The first track, 'Throw Your Hands Up', opens with a crash of urban grooves, rhythms and scratches, but it's just hip-hop by numbers: the sound used by tired old advertising executives who think they're 'down with the kids', making Colonel Sanders break-dance to sell his fried chicken. Maybe Kelly was trying to compare himself to Marvin Gaye – the Motown legend's classic album, *What's Going On*, kicks off with similar party noises. But the redundancy of the fake 'homies' is accentuated when the gentle, husky purity of Aaliyah's voice breaks in. She sounds young, but astonishingly mature, and her composure only breaks when she's forced to join in with the rap clichés. 'This is for the G's,' she growls, like a public speaker reading off an autocue.

'Back and Forth' is a distinct improvement. The lyrics - 'Tonight . . . oh, it's all right' – could have come straight out of a rhyming dictionary, but Aaliyah's performance is utterly convincing, not to say controversial. She

> *'I like to look sexy, but not out there sexy.'*

expresses the emotions of a young girl discovering the first stirrings of erotic desire, in a number some people felt was too hot and steamy for a young girl to perform. As one critic, Alexis Petridis, put it, 'songs like "No One Knows How to Love Me Quite the Way You Do" [are] innocuous enough by the bump 'n' grind standards of R&B, but faintly troubling when sung by a fourteen-year-old girl.'

The title track adds more fuel to the controversy, but the story it tells is ambiguous. 'Tonight we're gonna go all the way,' croons Aaliyah, and it sounds as if *she* is the dominant one, *she* is the one doing the reassuring, guiding a younger lover down the sexual

Aaliyah exudes down to earth glamour for a 1996 photo shoot.

'I've got a lot of things I want to do in my life and I'm not going to let anyone stop me.'

'I've had hard times and it says something about you if you can pull through it and come back.'

highway. The ability of such a young girl to take on the role of a sexually experienced seductress is a little disturbing. The lyrics, by R. Kelly, would have fitted his own erotic persona nicely. When put into the mouth of an underage girl, however, it almost seemed as if social and sexual mores were coming under attack. This was emphatically not cotton-candy R&B by numbers.

After such a challenging number comes 'Down with the Clique', macho hip-hop posturing over a cheesy, pseudo-Caribbean rhythm track. Kelly's egomania really goes to town here, as Aaliyah entreats, 'all the dolls in the house' to recognise how cool her mentor/songwriter/producer truly is.

Significantly perhaps, the best track on *Age Ain't Nothing but a Number* is the only one that Kelly didn't write. 'At Your Best You Are Love' is a cover version of a track originally written and recorded by the Isley Brothers on their 1976 album, *Harvest for the World*. (R. Kelly would later duet with Ron Isley on the single 'Down Low [Nobody Has To Know]' in 1996.) When contemporary soul or R&B artists cover classics from the Sixties or Seventies, the producer often insists on embellishing the track with frills to make it more 'urban' or relevant to a young, modern audience – similar to what the Fugees did to the Delfonics' solid gold 'Ready or Not'.

Kelly was wise enough to realise that the combination of Aaliyah and the Isleys didn't need any rapping, scratching or borrowed beats. The electric piano and wah-wah guitar cement the link to the Isleys' original, but it's Aaliyah's sublime, controlled performance that dominates – maybe a little old-fashioned, schmaltzy even, but so self-assured that it really doesn't matter. After all the contrived pop/rap of the previous tracks, the *a cappella* intro reminds us where Aaliyah came from – it's a sweet, soulful performance evoking her famous relative, Gladys Knight.

And then it's back to the R. Kelly Book Of Hip-Hop Clichés, as he borrows Melle Mel's classic rap on Chaka Khan's 'I Feel For You' for 'No One Knows How To Love Me Quite Like You Do' – an annoying blemish on an otherwise infectious slab of urban soul, enlivened by spunky girl-talk and Aaliyah's youthful enthusiasm. The track also nods backwards to earlier schools of R&B, incorporating a sample from 'Impeach the President' by Joe Liggins' funk combo the Honeydrippers.

The playful mood is carried into the next track, 'I'm So Into You', as the narrator's passion for a boy is conveyed via her rapping girlfriend: 'Aaliyah told me to tell you to call her' is her version of the classic teenage 'my friend likes you' tactic. (Say what you like about Kelly, but he understands the interaction between young girls.)

It's back to the ballads on 'Street Thing', with a Seventies-style synthesiser line that harks back to disco acts like Rose Royce and a rhythm similar to Kelly's 1997 smash hit, 'I Believe I Can Fly'. There's another lucky-dip into the history of black music on 'Young Nation' – the harmonica riff echoes Stevie Wonder, while the lyric is a reference to 'One Nation Under a Groove', the butt-shaking anthem by George Clinton's Funkadelic.

'Old School' is a mellow, yearning hymn of praise to the music Kelly had grown up with since childhood, and maybe an emotional longing to return to the old days. Once again Kelly muscles in, telling his own life story, 'trying to figure out how I could make my own record,' but it's a universal tale of nostalgia. The whole album is infused with the history of African-American music, from Ronald Isley to Run DMC, and 'Old School' cheerfully admits the fact.

Aaliyah's 'street but sweet' image was enhanced by modelling for designer Tommy Hilfiger, 1996.

'I'm Down' is, on the face of it, just another love song, but lines like 'I'm down with the way that you want me to be' do nothing to dispel the idea that Aaliyah is nothing but Kelly's marionette. It's a low-key, unsatisfying closer to an album that, for all its faults, was a showcase for R&B's newest, most incandescent star. (The CD also included two bonus tracks, the sweet, singalong 'The Thing I Like' and a more hard-edged remix of the 'Back and Forth' single.)

'People may try to manipulate you and control you, and those are the things you have to avoid.'

The general reaction of the critics was that Aaliyah was a new, shining talent, but that the album did not show her off to the best of her abilities. Danny Kelly in *Q* observed that 'much of Kelly's work recalls music made twenty years ago' and that, despite the artist's abilities, the finished product is little more than 'this year's flavour in coffee-table soul'. Most critics followed the same line of argument – Aaliyah had the potential to produce a classic album of modern, hip-hop-influenced soul, but her debut offering was not it.

Nevertheless, *Age Ain't Nothing but a Number* was a healthy commercial success, hitting number eighteen on the *Billboard* album chart. It achieved platinum status within four months of its release and spawned two top five singles ('Back and Forth' and 'At Your Best You Are Love'), both of which also went gold. *Entertainment Weekly* placed the young singer among the big hitters of R&B when it entreated its readers to 'imagine En Vogue packed into one teenage body and backed by hip-hop svengali R. Kelly and you have Aaliyah.'

But it wasn't just the sounds or the sales figures that grabbed the attention of the press. For Aaliyah wasn't just a fine singer, she was also beautiful, charismatic and a little mysterious. Add the brooding presence of R. Kelly to the mix, and there was plenty to keep the gossip columnists and celebrity hacks busy.

Unsurprisingly, much of the media reaction focused on Aaliyah's tender age. There's a double standard at work when it comes to young performers in the music

'I've always been someone that has had an affinity towards edgy things, towards kind of a darkside.'

industry. If the artist is male, like the pre-teen Michael Jackson when he and his brothers sang 'I Want You Back', or, from an earlier era, Frankie Lymon, he's seen as a precocious wunderkind and his grown-up love songs are *kinda cute*. But if the singer is a girl – think of Britney Spears or Vanessa Paradis – any implied physicality is seized on as morally suspect. Aaliyah's performance was unexceptional by the earthy standards of some R&B artists, but, from such a young performer, it was controversial.

There was also something bigger going down. The rumour was that R. Kelly's interest in his young protégée was rather more than professional. In fact, according to some sources, the couple were married – a reporter from black urban music magazine *Vibe* claimed to have found a marriage certificate issued in Cook County, Illinois. The reactions from the pair were inconsistent: from an evasive 'no comment' to outright denial, or a combination of the two. In Aaliyah's own words, 'I don't really comment on that because I know it's not true. When people ask me, I tell them, "Hey, don't believe all that mess. We're close and people took it the wrong way."' However, the pair added fuel to the fire by appearing publicly in carefully co-ordinated matching outfits. And Aaliyah, in a rare unguarded moment, once even joked that they were like an old married couple.

Celebrity relationships are always a godsend to the gossip columnists, but, if the rumours and insinuations were true, there would have been an additional reason for both parties to maintain discretion – Kelly was twelve years older than Aaliyah, and in most of the USA their match would have been illegal. The marriage licence uncovered by *Vibe* lists Aaliyah's age as eighteen, but on 31 August, 1994, the date recorded on the document, she was just fifteen years old. Sordid parallels could be drawn with the scandals surrounding pioneer rocker Jerry Lee Lewis and Bill Wyman of the Rolling Stones, both of whom caused media outrage by their relationships with very young girls.

'My family sat me down and told me, "You don't have any privacy. You really belong to the public."'

Aaliyah's aloofness from the rumours set the pattern for how she would handle press intrusion. Her image was already slightly mysterious – all moody gazes and dark glasses – but she took it even further, side-stepping virtually all enquiries about her private life. She'd seen how many young stars had found themselves centre-stage in a glossy freak show, and her unwillingness to open up – supported by the loyalty of her family and close friends – only added to her mystique. After the tragic events of summer 2001, it seems as if there are some things about Aaliyah that will never be known for sure. R. Kelly has always remained extremely reticent about what happened, not just out of concern for his own standing, but also, 'because Aaliyah is gone now and out of respect for her and her Mom and her Dad, I will not discuss Aaliyah.'

The rumours certainly raised the media profiles of both parties, but not in any way that would be helpful to their long-term careers. Everyone knew Aaliyah's name, but was it really a good thing if they knew her as Mrs R. Kelly, or – worse – as a piece of celebrity jailbait? The drama took its toll on Aaliyah who later admitted to the press, 'I was a novice . . . I had a lot to learn . . . There can be tumultuous times when you deal with something that is rough, but you just have to get through it.' But, with her family backing her all the way, Aaliyah was able to stand firm against the rumour mongers, her determination evident in an interview with the *Chicago Sun-Times*: 'I do see myself becoming my own artist. If you know your own style and you're sure of yourself, you can definitely overcome the whole protégé thing.' She never spoke out against Kelly either, summing up with the words, 'R Kelly is a wonderful producer and a wonderful artist. He's all good, but that time was very tense, so it's not really appropriate for us to see each other.'

Kelly himself would continue to be dogged by rumours even when Aaliyah was out of the picture, making financial settlements with two girls (both under sixteen) who filed civil cases against him in the late 1990s. These legal cases finally forced Aaliyah to admit there had been a marriage, however brief – in 1997, she asked the court to restrict access to official records of the wedding, to avoid becoming involved in the case of Tiffany Hawkins, one of the complainants. It turned out that the marriage was annulled in Michigan after a matter of weeks, when Aaliyah's real age came to light. Further serious scandal was to hit Kelly in late 2001, when a videotape surfaced, allegedly depicting him having sex with an underage girl (apparently a niece of the hip-hop performer Sparkle, yet another protegé of Kelly). This time, it wasn't just whispers, rumours and innuendo that were dogging him, and in June 2002 he was officially charged with possession of child pornography. At a court appearance that year, onlookers were shocked by his haggard appearance. And he has been candid about his problems, saying, 'There are things I'm trying to change. Being with the wrong crowd or being around a lot of women all the time. The success can get out of hand and it has gotten out of hand.' In the meantime, the scandal has seriously affected his career. Only time will tell of Kelly's guilt or innocence, and whether he will be able to move on from the allegations against him, and work through his problems. As Kelly puts it, 'Everybody's struggling with something.'

'I like to remember that God is in my heart and leading me the way through any setbacks.'

Even if she were to ignore the whispers, it soon became clear that Aaliyah would never be able to attain the success due to her if she was constantly in Kelly's long shadow. *Age Ain't Nothing But A Number* was a successful debut, but she was simply playing a role in a show directed by the all-powerful Mr Kelly. If she was going to emulate the success of her idols, the Houstons and the Streisands, Aaliyah would have to perform on her own terms.

So the relationship with R. Kelly, both personal and professional, came to an end. According to several sources, the split was provoked by Aaliyah's parents' fury at the illegitimate marriage. To this day, however, nobody in the pair's immediate circle of friends has ever confirmed that anything was going on beyond a close friendship. The closest her family ever came to acknowledging a formal union was when Michael Haughton, Aaliyah's father, said, 'It was a situation that happened. It's gone now. She's getting on with her life' – although, on another occasion, he dismissed the marriage rumour as 'a damn lie and the only guy who needed to stand up and tell the truth was Mr Kelly himself.'

Aaliyah , clearly bruised by the whole situation, concentrated on her studies for a time, back in *'I'm still young, I have no regrets.'* Detroit. But the lure of the bright lights would prove too strong. After a couple of years, she'd be back – free of R. Kelly, and shining brighter than ever.

The seventeen-year-old Aaliyah's strength and beauty, caught on camera during a 1996 shoot.

3: HOT LIKE FIRE

'Baby Girl, you got the whole world screaming.'

'Come To Give Love'

ALIYAH'S syllabus at the Detroit High School for the Fine and Performing Arts had given her a theoretical and practical grounding in many aspects of her chosen field. However, she wasn't the kind of performer who could just go into a studio with a mass of equipment and emerge months later with a hit record. Unlike a Prince or a Stevie Wonder, who handle the bulk of the songwriting and production, Aaliyah was a strictly interpretative singer. Aaliyah simply considered this a given part of her artistic identity: 'I've never written a song. I don't know if I'll ever really write a song. I've always been an interpreter. I act it out, so to speak on it personally I can't do.'

Since the rise of performer-songwriters like the Beatles, Bob Dylan and Smokey Robinson, a widespread critical prejudice against people who are 'only' singers has grown up, as if it places them only one small level above manufactured boy- and girl-bands. But some of the greatest singers of the 20th century, such as Frank Sinatra and Elvis Presley, never wrote anything of any significance (although Elvis's manager insisted he was co-credited for some of his greatest hits), and were by no means world-class instrumentalists. Their genius lay in selecting the great songs, and the collaborators most appropriate to their talents, and in their personal interpretation of those songs. The result is that classic recordings such as 'My Way' or 'Suspicious Minds' are now regarded as Sinatra or Presley songs, while the identities of the composers are known only to contestants on quiz shows.

While nobody could accuse Aaliyah of being a talentless showbiz puppet, she too need-ed top-class collaborators in the studio. With R. Kelly out of the picture, Aaliyah was look-ing people with both the musical imagination and technical know-how to use her vocal talents to their best advantage. As she put it, 'It's fun to be creative and innovative and come up with something crazy. So I needed people to work with who were not going to be afraid to take it to the left a bit.'

She clicked, personally and professionally, with a couple of hot young talents from the musical backwater of Virginia. Tim Mosley, known as Timbaland, had brought quirky Southern rhythms to hip-hop, often in collaboration with the rapper Magoo. He had also written some songs for the Jodeci album *Diary of a Mad Band* with a feisty lady called Melissa Elliott, a sometime member of the group Sista known as Missy. When Aaliyah's management approached him about bringing his left-field magic to their artist's second album, he took his homegirl into the studio for songwriting support and vocal arrangements. From the start Aaliyah impressed both Missy and Timbaland with not only her talent but her spirit. Said Missy, 'We'd sold no records. But from day one she treated us like we'd already sold two million. Her faith made us what we are today.' Aaliyah was similarly struck by Missy, 'When we met there was a bond that we established real quickly. A friendship formed and we built our studio relationship from that. We'll probably always work together.'

'I trust Tim totally: when he has a crazy track that he doesn't think anyone else will do he knows I'll try it.'

Tim and Missy worked on seven of the fifteen full-strength tracks on *One in a Million*, providing the crucial ingredient that set the album apart from its predecessor. For the first time, Aaliyah was both a musical contributor and collaborator, firing ideas off her studio crew for the first true Aaliyah album. As she said in an interview with *i-D*, 'With Tim, he knows I'll be the one that will try anything. He knows I'll go to a place with him that no-one else will go . . . I trust Tim totally; when he has a crazy track that he doesn't think anyone else will do, he knows that I'll try it.'

It wasn't only the music that had changed. The photographs in the inlay packaging for *One in a Million* portray a different Aaliyah from the uncomfortable pseudo-B-girl on *Age Ain't Nothing but a Number*, just two years earlier. She's out there on her own, no hovering, pimp-like daddy keeping watch. There are a couple of shots of her in baggy pants and sneakers, baring a honed midriff, but most of the images portray a sophisticated, well-dressed soul diva. (There's one sweet, downhome touch – at the end of the styling credits, Aaliyah's hair is attributed to Diane Hankerson, aka Mom.) But, classy as she looked, a grown-up image wasn't going to earn her any plaudits if the music couldn't cut it.

Like the first album, *One in a Million* kicks off with an unauthored slab of sound. But while the former album's 'Intro' was a confused mixture of musical snippets, 'Beats 4 da Streets' is like a spooky movie in miniature, dominated by Missy's theatrical presence. It reflected the album's sense of drama, and Aaliyah's penchant for not just laying down vocal tracks but giving a complete performance.

The first fully-fledged track is 'Hot Like Fire', which shows what a difference two years have made. With the more sexually-explicit tracks on the debut album, the listener was painfully aware of a young girl mouthing grown-up sentiments. But here, lyrics like 'ya got me meltin' like a sundae' sound sexy rather than sordid. This is a young woman in love with life, feeling the first flushes of passion at its most intense.

The title track takes the heat down a few degrees: it's love, not lust, that provides the theme. The lyrics are goofy, lovey-dovey, straight out of a Valentine card ('you give me a

Aaliyah combined contemporary style with classic glamour. (Teen People, 1999)

'I'm not gonna go too far but I'm gonna be me and I'll embrace my sexiness for sure.'

really good feeling all day long') but, like any well-trained actress, Aaliyah can bestow credibility on the dumbest of lines, aided in this instance by a moody, percussion-heavy production, accentuated with turntable scratches and old-school synth stabs.

'A Girl Like You' shows off the skills of Naughty By Nature. This New Jersey hip-hop crew hit it big in 1991 with the *double entendre*-laden 'O.P.P.', and became one of the few Nineties rap outfits to consistently combine underground credibility with sustained commercial success. Their MC Treach weighs in with some trademark rapping, and there's also a classy sample from the golden age of jazz-funk: 'Summer Madness', as laid down by Kool and the Gang on their 1974 album *Light of Worlds*.

'If Your Girl Only Knew' is a classic piece of Missy Elliott 'girl power'. Aaliyah is hit on by a two-timing guy, but realises the truth of the situation: if he's prepared to do that to one girl, he'd have no problem doing it to another – 'it's dumb to put up with you.' Looking out for your sisters can also be a better deal for yourself.

One link with Aaliyah's first album is in the choice of a cover version. Once again she went to the Isley Brothers songbook, this time borrowing 'Choosey Lover' from their 1983 album *Between the Sheets*. No sentimental romantic ballad, its honest dissection of infidelity and disillusionment has Aaliyah trilling, 'Thought I had a love but I was kidding myself, baby.'

'I needed people to work with who were not going to be afraid to take it to the left a bit.'

As the new subtitle ('Old School/New School') suggests, it's a clever culture clash of Eighties soul/funk with the brave new world of digital hip-hop/R&B production techniques. For most of the track, producers Vincent Herbert and Craig King provide a gentle, slightly old-fashioned groove, before the conventional instrumentation (including a note-perfect evocation of Ernie Isley's searing guitar lines by Michael J. Powell) disappears, to be replaced by dubby, elastic bass and clicky percussion, with Aaliyah freestyling over the top. Aaliyah delivers a vocal that perfectly expresses happy contentment after a period of anguish.

'Choosey Lover' is followed by another cover version. On Marvin Gaye's 'Got To Give It Up', Aaliyah is really playing with the big boys. It's one of the holy relics of Seventies soul, a hymn to sex, love and enjoyment. The definitive version, on Gaye's 1977 album *Live at the London Palladium*, clocks in at just under twelve minutes, raising the song to the level of a religious rite. It was one of the pieces that set a blueprint for the male soul titans of the Eighties and Nineties, such as Lionel Richie, Luther Vandross, and, indeed, R. Kelly. So for a seventeen-year-old babe from Detroit to take it on might seem brave at best, or like something approaching sacrilege at worst – though at least the debt to the great Marvin was made explicit in the promotional video, where Aaliyah dances with his image.

But once again, Herbert and King updated the sound while keeping true to the spirit of the original. Their secret ingredient was Slick Rick. Born Ricky Walters in South London, 1965, he's a veteran of the Bronx hip-hop scene in the late Seventies and early Eighties, and a major influence on the movement that became known as gangsta rap. His pimp style, topped off with an eyepatch, his brushes with the law (he served a jail sentence in the early Nineties after a shooting incident) and songs like his breakthrough hit, 'Treat Her Like a

*Aaliyah took street style and made it her own. (*Seventeen *magazine, January 1997)*

Prostitute', made him a controversial figure in the hip-hop and R&B communities.

On the new version of 'Got To Give It Up' he plays a parody of his own gangsta persona. He's trying to be a laidback playa, chugging Hennessy brandy and Crystal champagne, but his bubble of cool is popped when Aaliyah walks into the party. Ms Haughton's vocal takes on Marvin Gaye's own angelic qualities, as if she's floating above Rick's faintly ridiculous antics. (Maybe Rick was playing the role of R. Kelly.)

'4 Page Letter' turns the heat down a few notches, and we suddenly remember Aaliyah was still a teenager in high school when she was recording the album. The lyrics – 'I'm sending him a four page letter and I enclosed it with a kiss' – hark back to the golden age of innocent boyfriend/girlfriend pop songs like the Marvelettes' 'Please Mr Postman', while the tight female harmonies echo TLC and En Vogue. This track, from the Timbaland/Missy hit factory, mixes cool sophistication with adolescent yearning.

> *'It's fun to be creative and innovative and come up with something crazy.'*

A burst of minimalist urban funk ushers in 'Everything's Gonna Be Alright'. The producer of this cut is Rodney Jerkins, a protégé of swing-beat legend Teddy Riley who was only a year older than Aaliyah herself. He got his first production credit on an album by soul-pop singer Casserine in 1994, when he was just sixteen. Within a few years, he would be one of the biggest players on the urban music scene, producing Michael Jackson and Mary J. Blige, and giving credibility lessons to the likes of Britney Spears, N'Sync and the Spice Girls. The track is a cool party anthem, where everybody namechecks everybody else.

It's *luuurve* song time again with 'Giving You More' by J. Dibbs, who won his spurs writing songs for beauty queen/*Penthouse* model/soul diva Vanessa Williams. The track features some effective multi-tracking, as Aaliyah goes into gospel-style improvisation over her own soft, angelic backing vocals – what Timbaland later described as 'that hummingbird sound'.

'I Gotcha Back' is the work of Jermaine Dupri. Yet another one-time child prodigy (he danced onstage with Motown megadiva Diana Ross at age ten), Dupri went on to write and produce for TLC and Mariah Carey. Less to his credit, he was the mastermind behind kiddy duo Kriss Kross, whose 'Jump Jump' was one of the more irritating chart hits of the early Nineties. With barefaced lyrical borrowings from old chestnuts like 'You'll Never Walk Alone' and 'You've Got a Friend', it's not the most original track on the album but still a good vehicle for the sassy Aaliyah Mark Two – secure enough in her own femininity to admit how she uses her feminine wiles: 'it's not the things I say, but the way I say it that keeps them locked down.'

Aaliyah was facing up to one of the key problems that has to be addressed by any entertainer who grows up in public – how to mark the shift of persona from romantically inclined teenager to sexually confident adult. Should they act like Michael Jackson, an asexual pre-teen in his forties – or risk the backlash that actress Lisa Bonet, the teenage daughter in *The Cosby Show*, faced when she appeared in an intense, blood-drenched sex scene in the 1987 film *Angel Heart*? Aaliyah's implied sexuality had been a controversial ingredient of her first album. Now she had more autonomy as a performer, she was able to express her needs in a more explicit – but never X-rated – manner. As she put it, 'I'm

A demure Aaliyah holds still for the camera in Seventeen *magazine, January 1997.*

not gonna go too far but I'm gonna be me and I'll embrace my sexiness for sure.' In fact two things were sure, Aaliyah wanted to make the transition, and she especially wanted to move on from the image moulded by R Kelly. Her experiences with him had cemented her ideas about being a public figure and what kind of image she wanted to project. She had grown up. 'I've no problem being a sex symbol' she now said, 'I'm cool with that. I just want to keep it classy.'

This slab of raunch is followed by 'Never Givin' Up', the last of three productions by V. H. and Craig King. It's a modern R&B ballad about contemplating a relationship once the first flush of passion has gone, slightly hampered by the strangulated duet vocals of the producers' protégé, Tavarius Polk.

'Heartbroken' is an anthem of steely resignation to life with a man who's obviously bad for his woman, over an eerie Hammond organ line. (It also features a sample from 'Inside My Love', a track from Minnie Riperton's 1975 album *Adventures in Paradise*. Riperton, who recorded the classic 'Loving You', died of cancer in 1979 at the age of only 31.)

'Never Comin' Back' is a ballsy female anthem, much closer to Missy's later Miss Demeanour persona. 'I'm packin' up and you can hit the road, Jack,' declares Aaliyah, a warning to potential heartbreakers everywhere. Missy's own talent is let off the leash on 'Ladies in da

'To be able to act and sing now is the fulfillment of all that I've wanted to do.'

House', a truer girl power anthem than anything the Spice Girls ever did. Aaliyah slips in a subtle reference to Donna Summer's strutting disco anthem 'Bad Girls', then Missy takes the spotlight for a feisty little rap ('delicious/make three wishes/dirty like dishes'), a template for her future career. Timbaland chips in with a neat little parody of 1970s Isaac (*Shaft*) Hayes, now better known as Chef on *South Park*. But this one, as the title makes clear, is a females-only zone.

At this stage in her career, Aaliyah was boxed in by the segregated nature of the American music industry. In the USA, most radio stations follow tight programme formats that let the advertisers know what sort of market they're reaching – Top 40, country, Latin, urban – and any musician who wants airplay has to wear the correct label. The system is made even more rigid by America's uneasy attitude to race. Well over 100 years since President Lincoln abolished slavery, many blacks and whites live totally segregated lives. Gangsta rap managed to break down a few barriers, when fourteen-year-old white boys got into NWA and others, but the style of sophisticated R&B performed by Aaliyah was still perceived as, in the words of the T-shirt, 'a black thing . . . you wouldn't understand.' Those soul artists, like Whitney Houston, who crossed over to attract the white audience, did so on the back of big, soaring ballads. Which is where Diane Warren came in.

Warren's songs have been recorded by performers as diverse as Celine Dion, Tina Turner, Ricky Martin, Ace of Base and Aerosmith, As a songwriter, she provokes polarised reactions: people either have her songs played at their wedding, or feel the urge to shoot the radio when one of them comes round for the seventh time that day. But there's no doubting her commercial appeal, or her ability to create a song that displays a singer's vocal skills to their best advantage.

Aaliyah strikes a pose for Seventeen *magazine, January 1997.*

'The One I Gave My Heart To' isn't a copperbottomed Warren classic of the stature of 'I Don't Wanna Miss a Thing' or 'How Do I Live', but it was a clear signal as to where Aaliyah's career was headed. If Whitney Houston could cross over in the Eighties and Nineties, Aaliyah was going to be the crossover star of the new millennium.

'Sensual is being in touch with your sensual self.'

By the time the album plays out with 'Came to Give Love', it's clear that Aaliyah had fulfilled her early promise. Her ability to combine pop, soul, R&B and hip-hop, to create music that was both artistically credible and commercially viable, marked her out as a rare talent. And this was only her second album, the first one where she had any level of creative control. The world, to coin a cliché, hadn't seen nothin' yet. This was exactly what Timbaland and Missy had set out to do, collaborate closely with Aaliyah, but give her much freer rein than R Kelly ever had. Said Missy, 'I felt like if she was venturing to do something on her own, why give her what R Kelly gave her? Because then she might as well have asked R Kelly to do the album.'

The three clearly had a great time making the *One In A Million*. Said Timbaland, 'Working with Aaliyah in the studio was like being in the funhouse', while Aaliyah enthused, 'When we work together it is always fun . . . When we go into a studio it is like going into a club.'

But the trio had never lost sight of their aim to branch out and experiment. As Timbaland said, 'she liked to go to the far left like I did.' And for Aaliyah, the most rewarding part of the process was the fact that, 'As I work with new people, I like to pick up all these different sounds.'

One In A Million was a team effort that impressed the critics, who immediately recognised the extent to which the singer had developed her art over two short years. Dave Roberts in *Q* praised Aaliyah's 'smooth, sweetly seductive vocal', with the caveat, 'over the course of fifteen, often overlong tracks, self-indulgence turns into sugary schmaltz once too often.'

The *CMJ New Music Report* also noted the occasional lapse into smooth blandness, especially on Jermaine Dupri's contribution, but summed up with, 'Sure to achieve many well-deserved accolades, *One in a Million* is one of the year's best R&B records.'

Initially it looked as if *One in a Million* would struggle to match the success of Aaliyah's debut. Individual tracks achieved a healthy amount of airplay, with the title track topping the *Billboard* R&B singles airplay chart for six weeks at the beginning of 1997. But none of the singles made it to the top five in the sales charts: 'The One I Gave My Heart To' reached number nine; 'If Your Girl Only Knew' made number ten, 'One in a Million' stalled at number thirteen; while '4 Page Letter' entered the bowels of the chart at number forty and departed the following week.

But it's the Britneys and the N'Syncs who worry about singles chart positions. For any act that want to escape from the ghetto of marshmallow pop, it's album sales that matter. And *One in a Million* was slowly but surely shifting units. Certified gold in October 1996, it made platinum in February of the following year, and double platinum by the summer.

The Source magazine recognised, 'Aaliyah is ready to showcase her mature side.' It was certainly apparent that she was becoming a grown-up artist, appealing to a wide constituency of fans. She'd managed the transition from child star to serious performer with aplomb. But few of the thousands who snapped up *One in a Million* could have guessed the direction that her career was going to take next.

A sultry Aaliyah during a Honey *magazine photo-shoot, April 2000.*

4: THAT SOMEBODY

'This is something I've wanted to do
for a very long time . . .'

'Come To Give Love'

THE PURISTS MAY COMPLAIN, but image is crucial to popular music. Elvis Presley wasn't just a great singer – it was also his smouldering good looks, his lop-sided sneer, and his wiggling pelvis that made him the King of Rock 'n' Roll. Motown stars like Marvin Gaye, the Supremes and the Temptations were great singers, backed by fantastic musicians, performing timeless songs. But they were also seriously sharp dressers, and, under the instruction of choreographers like Cholly Atkins, their moves were so cool that everyone wanted to copy them.

Image became even more important in the early Eighties, when the promotional video became a tool for stimulating record sales. Hits such as 'Thriller' by Michael Jackson drew as

'I would love to get into acting . . .
That would be really exciting to be a
jack of all trades.'

much attention to the talent, technology and money invested in the video as they did to the song and its performance. One of the most important developments in the promotional video industry was the birth of MTV, a television station devoted entirely to music videos. If your promo went into heavy rotation on MTV, it was worth the same as going on the A-list of thousands of radio stations across the planet.

While the promo video could often be used to sell artists with little talent for performing, there were some who were adept in both fields. Just because Jackson appeared in a groundbreaking, multi-million-dollar video extravaganza, it didn't mean he couldn't write and perform great songs. Artists as diverse as Prince, Eurythmics and Run DMC made videos as complements to their songs, not replacements for them.

'I work every day. Ev-e-ry day. I want to knock people out.'

And so it was with Aaliyah. People bought her records because of her extraordinary voice, but the fact that she was a beautiful young woman, with something of an air of mystery about her, didn't do sales any harm either. The guarded air she cultivated in interviews, and on the artwork of her CDs, was elaborated on in her promo videos. Her natural reserve, bought to the fore by her teenage scandal, combined with her unabashed beauty to create an image that was darkly alluring, and perfect for the camera. And in video director Paul Hunter, Aaliyah found a new collaborator with whom she could explore the darker, sexier side of her image, and start making the transition from singer to all round star. In an interview for *Echoes*, Aaliyah elaborated: 'I've always had a sexy side. I'm 22 years old and a young adult and that will definitely shine through in the songs to the videos, to how the songs will be when I tour.'

In the video made by Paul Hunter for *One in a Million*, she moves through a series of apocalyptic, *Mad Max*-style sets, her clothing and appearance changing with every frame. Where some performers appear as just another piece of scenery in their videos, Aaliyah was part of the action, a full participant in the world Hunter created for her (even if it didn't make any coherent sense). She wasn't just performing – she was acting.

This is the point at which most rock stars are advised to take a long holiday. Many – Mick Jagger, Prince, Madonna, Jon Bon Jovi, et al – are captivating and charismatic on stage, in the studio, and in their videos. But all too often their egos insist they take on the discipline of dramatic acting, with all the demands of the script and interaction with properly-trained thespians.

But Aaliyah, with her grounding in the performing arts, could talk the talk and walk the walk. Hunter noted this: 'She's just very comfortable in front of the camera. When the camera is on she just

'From childhood I knew I wanted to be an actress and a dancer: a total entertainer.'

lights up. She loves performing. She lives for this kind of work.' It was time to follow in the footsteps of all-round entertainers like Sammy Davis Jr. and Barbra Streisand, who could act, sing, dance or direct, constantly surprising their audiences. It was time to go to Hollywood.

Aaliyah had already been credited on several movies without ever stepping in front of the cameras. Back in 1994, at the time she was making her first album, her song 'The Thing I Like' was featured on the soundtrack of the action comedy *A Low Down Dirty Shame*. A breezy song of young love with a catchy synth riff, it juxtaposed Aaliyah's soft soul vocals with insistent rapping, like a grab bag of contemporary black music.

Two years later, 'Are You Ready?' featured in the unlikely basketball drama *Sunset Park* (just how unlikely is indicated by the casting of Rhea Perlman, the waitress from *Cheers*, as a hoop coach). But it was in 1997, with the release of the animated movie *Anastasia*, that Aaliyah's name made the pages of *Variety* as well as *Billboard*.

The lush ballad 'Journey to the Past' earned considerably better reviews than the movie itself, which was an old-fashioned attempt to copy the success of Disney's animated blockbusters. In fact, it earned a nomination for Best Song at the 1998 Academy Awards. It didn't win – steamrollered by Celine Dion's 'My Heart Will Go On', from *Titanic* – but it earned Aaliyah the chance to sing at the awards ceremony. Hollywood's movers and shakers got to see her poise and confidence while performing before an international TV audience of millions.

She also contributed to another high-profile soundtrack in 1998, working with Timbaland on the street-smart 'Are You That Somebody?' for Eddie Murphy's raucous reworking of the children's classic *Dr Dolittle*. It revitalised her credibility in the singles charts, reaching the number two position, but still left Aaliyah's own Hollywood ambitions unfulfilled. As she said, 'From childhood I knew I wanted to be an actress and a dancer: a total entertainer. I would sit in a movie theatre, thinking "One day I'll be on that silver screen."'

Her chance finally came with *Romeo Must Die* in 1999, made in Vancouver, Canada, with one of the hottest international action stars. Jet Li already had a CV full of Hong Kong movies such as *Once Upon a Time in China*, and was being tipped as the heir to Bruce Lee as a martial arts icon. He first caught the eye of western multiplex audiences in the fourth instalment of the *Lethal Weapon* franchise, but this was the first time he had top billing in a Hollywood film.

As the title suggests, *Romeo Must Die* borrows heavily from Shakespeare's classic tale of forbidden love, *Romeo and Juliet*. The twist this time is that the warring 'families' are Asian-American and African-American gangs, while Han Sing (Jet Li) and Trish O'Day (Aaliyah) answer the call of mutual attraction despite their families being at each other's throats. Aaliyah's role was a little passive: without the necessary years of martial arts training, she wasn't able to match Li's fist-flashing, jaw-kicking antics. But her background in performance gave her the confidence to take on new challenges, and she managed to get a few kicks in during the frenetic fight scenes.

'What I like about Trish is that she's tough,' said Aaliyah after filming. 'She's independent. She doesn't take anything off anybody. But at the same time, she loves her family. She's got a sweet side. So I felt I could play her, and people could get into her. It would be realistic to people, being that people know me as Aaliyah, the artist – there is this image that I have. I wanted to make the right transition and have people understand where I was going, and I felt Trish embodied all of that.'

As Li described to CNN, 'When I first met her, she asked "Jet, can you teach me some martial and kung fu stuff? I want to fight in the movie."' Aaliyah refused stunt doubles, explaining, 'I wanted the audience to be like, "wow, she actually got up there and is kicking some butt."' Aaliyah identified with her character – 'She is tough, she is independent, she is edgy, she gets involved in the action,' she said with evident approval – and coped admirably with the more intimate scenes. Some critics claimed she acted her slightly wooden co-star off the screen, particularly in an emotive scene where she had to shed tears. As she recalled in an MTV interview, this scene was by far the most difficult. 'It was a very depressing day. The whole day, I had to really touch a lot of pain, things that happened to me in my life. My grandmother passed away two years ago, so I thought about her. It was a draining and depressing day, but it brought those tears out.'

Movie reviewers were dismissive of *Romeo Must Die*, comparing it unfavourably with

Above: Aaliyah discusses her next move with Jet Li, during rehearsals for Romeo Must Die. *Opposite: Aaliyah with Jet Li at the premiere of* Romeo Must Die, *May 2000.*

authentic Hong Kong action movies, such as Jet Li's earlier work, and groundbreaking Hollywood movie *The Matrix*, which had redefined martial arts cinema by the use of jaw-dropping special effects. *Empire* magazine called it 'lumpy, derivative stuff' and Roger Ebert in the *Chicago Sun-Times* felt that, apart from a dumb plot, bad script and unconvincing action scenes, 'no great romantic chemistry is generated between the young lovers'. But such critical coolness didn't affect box office takings – the movie made $24.6 million in its first week in North American cinemas.

There wasn't much point in having a rising young music star on the cast if she didn't make a contribution to the soundtrack. As Jet Li kicked seven shades of crap out of the bad guys, Aaliyah's tunes were complemented by the cream of modern R&B, including Destiny's Child, Ginuwine, Joe, and her old buddy Timbaland. But it was Ms Haughton who contributed most, laying down four of the tracks on the soundtrack album. Timbaland and Missy Elliott were on hand in the studio to bring out the best in Aaliyah. There was also assistance from another of Timbaland's protegés, the talented Static, who provided most of the lyrics.

'Try Again' is an edgy slice of electro-R&B, imposing Aaliyah's luscious, multi-tracked vocals on top of a hiccoughing, stuttering beat – like Destiny's Child in a sulk. Aaliyah was already expert in interpreting love songs and sad ballads, now she was expanding her range to encompass urban paranoia. The fourteen-year-old girl on *Age Ain't Nothing but a Number* was just playing at being 'from the street'. The new, *sooo cool* Aaliyah was so street

that molten tarmac ran through her veins.

'Try Again' was the song that convinced the critics that the Aaliyah/Timbaland team were a cut above the R&B mainstream. Toby Manning in *Q* called it 'an acid bath bubbling beneath a seductive hook', while *The Guardian*'s Alexis Petridis labelled it, 'one of the most remarkable and forward-thinking pop singles of 2000'. It was a commercial as well as a critical hit, matching 'Are You That Somebody?' by reaching the number two spot on the *Billboard* chart. (The soundtrack itself earned a platinum disc and reached third place on the albums chart.)

'I would sit in a movie theatre, thinking "One day I'll be on that silver screen."'

Aaliyah's next track, 'Come Back in One Piece', is a duet with one of her co-stars in the movie. The Yonkers, New York MC DMX (born Earl Simmons) is a bad boy of hip-hop. With his debut album, the multi-platinum selling *It's Dark and Hell Is Hot*, he became one of the most prominent figures on the post-Tupac 'n' Biggie hip-hop landscape. His collaboration with Aaliyah is constructed around a bassline, sampled from 'Sir Nose D'Voidoffunk', a ten-minute track on Parliament's 1977 album *Funkentelechny vs. the Placebo Syndrome*. Just as George Clinton – the deranged mastermind behind Parliament and their sister band, Funkadelic – proved, it's when music cross-breeds and spawns mutations that it gets really exciting. When DMX's rough rap barking contrasts with Aaliyah's elegant pop sighs, it's a classic response to the purists who believe two styles of music can never successfully come together.

'Are You Feelin' Me?' arrives on a flying carpet of Middle Eastern sounds, adding another sonic dimension. Aaliyah's vocal is compressed and distressed, sounding as if she's biting the mic in frustration as she snaps at Missy Elliott's tough-talking lyrics. The last in this quartet of superlative cuts is 'I Don't Wanna', a yearning song about the breakdown of a relationship, enlivened by some nifty acoustic guitar fills and rumbling percussion. Overall, the soundtrack was a more impressive snapshot of urban culture clash than the movie itself, and it proved that Aaliyah belonged among R&B's biggest hitters.

'The role was the first time I had to do a little love scene, which I was very nervous about.'

In the same way that she was relegated to a supporting role in her own first album, *Romeo Must Die* was not the vehicle to show Aaliyah's talents at their fullest. It was her calling card to the Hollywood hotshots, a demonstration of her versatility. She wasn't just a singer taking advantage of her fame to dabble in another medium – she was a genuine movie actress. And to develop this multifaceted talent was the realisation of Aaliyah's long held dream.

Her next film gave her more of a chance to flex her acting muscles, even though it granted less screen time than her role in *Romeo Must Die*. Anne Rice's hugely successful series of novels about the vampire Lestat had already been translated to the big screen in

Aaliyah gets into character with Stuart Townsend, her co-star in Queen of the Damned.

*'I had to put my
shyness to the side and be Akasha.'*

Opposite: Aaliyah discusses a scene with co-star Stuart Townsend. Above: Aaliyah receives instruction from Queen of the Damned *director Michael Rymer.*

*'Akasha is this very regal, statuesque being, but
she's crazy.'*

Aaliyah and co-star Stuart Townsend in their love scene.

Interview with the Vampire, where Rice's predatory anti-hero was portrayed by diminutive megastar Tom Cruise. In Michael Rymer's *Queen of the Damned*, Lestat was to be portrayed by the less starry (but considerably taller) Stuart Townsend.

Townsend may have had the biggest part, but Aaliyah was given the title role (and the juiciest character) as Queen Akasha, a snarling, writhing, 6,000-year-old Egyptian vampire queen, flashing savage fangs and a profoundly sexy body with equal aplomb. As Aaliyah

'As a character, she's very manipulative and very sexual.'

described it, 'she's this very regal, statuesque being, but she's crazy.'

During filming, in Australia, director Rymer described the young woman in the role of the glamorous villainess as 'the sweetest, kindest, easiest-going person.' He wanted to make the creaky old vampire genre hip and relevant to a young, street-smart audience – much the same audience that made up Aaliyah's core fanbase, her casting being no coincidence. 'If *Interview with the Vampire* was Anne Rice in the style of Merchant Ivory,' said Rymer, 'our attempt was to do Anne Rice in the style of *Trainspotting*.'

The role of Akasha was, of course, light years away from Aaliyah's own personality, which made the project more challenging – and more fun. 'She's a bad, bad girl,' she said. 'She's evil. Totally evil. I've always been drawn to the darker side of things. I've loved vampire films ever since I was little. *The Lost Boys*, Kiefer Sutherland, mmm . . . When I read the script, straight away I knew I had to go after it.'

Clearly, Aaliyah was drawn towards the proverbial 'dark side.' On the surface this seems at odds with the upstanding 'street but sweet' image she cultivated. But if we look further, we see that as a musician she had already demonstrated a willingness to explore uncharted realms and transcend musical genres. Similarly, as a fledgling actress in her videos she was keen to take risks and play with her image. In short, as an entertainer she was open to experimentation; fully able to embrace the light and dark inherent in humanity.

And as a person, she was honest about her own individual brand of 'darkness', and how this lent to her air of mystique. In an interview with *i-D* magazine, she stated, 'I do think I'm a difficult person to know; it takes me a long time to feel comfortable and even open up to somebody. I'm very reserved and I can be soooo secretive.' At another point she made a more sinister declaration, 'Well, maybe I am a vampire. I mean how could you

'When I get onstage or in front of the camera, I transform into a different person.'

know? How could anyone know?'

All we know is that since her death many of Aaliyah's words and actions have taken on an eerie quality, as if they foretell her fate. Yet in life, they were the product of a strong young woman exploring every aspect of her character and craft. And this outlook served her well playing such a multi-faceted role in *Queen of the Damned*. As she explained, 'It took a lot to bring [the character] to life . . . I worked with an accent coach and we came up with a hybrid of American and Egyptian. Then I also worked with a choreographer to get the movement of vampires down, especially her because she's the queen and very statuesque. She's very evil, extremely powerful, and she's a bit of a brat because she's so young. She's used to getting what she wants. So it was a real challenge for me to play all those sides to her.'

However, while critics had been dismissive of *Romeo Must Die*, they really let rip on *Queen of the Damned*. Aaliyah was spared the worst of the vitriol, as most acclaimed her as the best thing in an otherwise lousy movie – tragically, however, she would never know her performance was acclaimed for soaring above the weak screenplay and direction.

'Aaliyah is a brittle, voracious goddess, a memorable presence in a tiny role,' said Wendy Ide in London listings magazine *Time Out*. Rob Blackwelder in *Splicedwire* was even more emphatic, claiming she 'absolutely transcends the screen and fills the whole theatre with her presence. She dominates this incongruous vampire flick with her chilling allure.' Many felt that she was wasted in the role. Gary Thompson in the *Philadelphia Daily News* complained that the movie 'makes sorry use of Aaliyah in her one and only starring role – she does little here but point at things that explode into flame.' Cynthia Fuchs in *Popmatters* took a similar line: 'Aaliyah sings not a note, and is left only with three or four scenes in which she must utter silly, exclamation-pointed dialogue through her big false teeth.'

Anthony Quinn, in English paper *The Independent*, summed up the reviewers' consensus: 'I assume the only reason this didn't go straight to the video graveyard is the presence of the late R&B star Aaliyah as the eponymous royal. She cuts an imperious figure, though it's hardly a pleasant epitaph to her career.'

Meanwhile, the soundtrack, masterminded by the crown prince of woe, Korn's Jonathan Davis, is given over to the tortured rock bellowings of Linkin Park's Chester

Bennington, Marilyn Manson, the Deftones and other alt-metal stalwarts. It fits the gothic machinations of the plot (Lestat is reincarnated as a diabolical rock star), but having Aaliyah singing in character might have livened up the film a little. It was a wasted opportunity – although working on a project with such heavy rock overtones seems to have influenced Aaliyah in the last months of her life. Her listening broadened to include the industrial metal of Trent Reznor's Nine Inch Nails, and a collaboration was supposedly on the cards. As she said in an interview with the UK's *Daily Telegraph*, 'I think Trent Reznor's dope!' Aaliyah and Trent did meet at an MTV awards ceremony and continued talking by phone about a possible collaboration. Said Aaliyah, 'He's a really nice person and extremely talented, so maybe we'll be able to collaborate. I think our sounds would really mesh well, so I'll bring a

'I've always been drawn to the darker side of things.'

little something to do the table, he'll bring something to the table and we'll see how it works.'

In fact, coming from a musical family, Aaliyah had always appreciated a wide range of music, which made her keen to incorporate as many styles as possible into her own work. In this way she would produce a uniquely dark vision of R&B. When asked by one interviewer how her musical tastes had changed over the years, she responded, 'I listen to a lot of the same artists I listened to when I was younger: Stevie [Wonder] and Sade. As I got older I got into alternative styles after my brother turned me on to them: Nine Inch Nails, Korn, Oasis and I started to check out things that I wouldn't have and returned to some that I did: Luther Vandross, Johnny Mathis!'

While Aaliyah had taken a brief hiatus from music to concentrate on breaking into movies, the industry was also beginning to recognise her as a major star. In 1999, 'Are You That Somebody?' received a Grammy nomination and two Soul Train Lady of Soul Award nominations (for the song itself and

At the MTV Video Music Awards in 2000 Aaliyah presents her own urban twist on classic Hollywood glamour.

its video); in 2000, 'Try Again' earned the same nominations, while Aaliyah was nominated for a prestigious Image Award from the National Association for the Advancement of Coloured People (NAACP). 'Are You That Somebody?' earned two MTV nominations (Best R&B Video and Best Video from a Film) in 1999, while in the following year 'Try Again' won awards in two categories (Best Female Video and Best Video from a Film). It also took two nominations at the *Billboard* Music Video Awards.

There was talk that Aaliyah would soon combine the two threads of her career in a movie about legendary jazz musician Miles Davis – entitled *Some Kind of Blue*, after one of his most famous recordings, and set during the 1958 Newport Jazz Festival. It remains unclear how far plans had gone on this project, but her other proposed film role was set to propel her into the big league of movie stardom.

The Matrix was one of the most groundbreaking movies of the 1990s. Combining thrilling martial arts sequences, paranoid science-fiction and startling special effects, the Wachowski Brothers' movie managed the tricky triple whammy of critical, cult and commercial success. The economic madhouse that is Hollywood dictated a sequel or two, so *The Matrix Reloaded* and *The Matrix Revolutions* were soon at the planning stage. One of the most popcorn-dropping aspects of the first movie had been the kung fu acrobatics of the character Trinity (Carrie-Ann Moss). By early 2001, word had it that Aaliyah, who had proved her fight skills in *Romeo Must Die*, had been signed to play the part of Zee, a feisty female character in the virtual reality neverland of the Matrix. There was no indication whether the character was to be a heroine, like Trinity, or an Akasha-style villainess. Either way, it seemed Aaliyah's credibility as an actress was assured. Aaliyah felt this too. And her talent was matched only by her ambition. She set her sights high and thought long-term, telling one interviewer about her hopes for future collaborations: 'There's so many people I admire and would love to work with. I'd love to work with Gwyneth Paltrow, I think she's amazing. And someone whom I've admired since I was young is Morgan Freeman. So at some point in my career if I have that opportunity, that would be really great.'

But, of course, it was not to be. (In 2002, it was announced that the part of Zee would be taken by Nona Gaye, the daughter of soul legend Marvin Gaye – whose 'Got To Give It Up' was covered so brilliantly by Aaliyah on *One in a Million*.) Any consideration of Aaliyah's career is overshadowed by the spectre of unfulfilled potential. Would she have made it as a fully-fledged movie star? All of her screen time could fit onto a single VHS tape, with room to spare. However, even if only for a short while, she was able to successfully step out beyond the boundaries of the recording studio. Her fans can only be thankful for whatever she left behind.

5: I CAN BE

'People expect so much from me, I'm always conscious of being different.'

Aaliyah, interviewed by *i-D*, summer 2001

As Aaliyah came into her twenties, she felt more secure about her own sexuality. It's unlikely she would have morphed into a foul-mouthed Foxy Brown, or a boob-flashing Li'l Kim, but the sensuality bubbling under the surface was due to be uncorked. The tomboy of the mid-Nineties was no more. 'There was a time back in the day when you'd have to prise me into a dress,' she told *i-D*. 'I guess I've just grown up a little.' As she said to *Teen People* magazine, 'Every woman wants to feel sexy. It's empowering.'

Aaliyah hinted at this suggestive yet discreet eroticism in *Queen of the Damned*. When she was in Australia, making the movie, she became fascinated with snakes and all their associations with the dark side of human sexuality. These connections have existed for thousands of years, linking the myth of Eve's temptation in the Garden of Eden with the suicide of Cleopatra (the latter clearly a role model for Queen Akasha). The father of psycho-analysis, Sigmund Freud, said that the

'If God gave you the talent you should go for it!'

phallic shape of snakes made them both frightening and enticing to adolescent girls discovering their sexuality. As if in verification, the first promo video for Aaliyah's new album (specifically the track 'We Need a Resolution') made full use of their slithery, suggestive power, the performer exuding raw eroticism as five huge pythons writhe around her scantily clad body.

As she later explained to *Pride*, 'I have thought about getting some [snakes] since touching them. I like that firmness and softness. Ooh, amazing! . . . a snake to me sug-

'Every woman wants to feel sexy. It's empowering.'

gests potency and power. I love to feel one sliding through my fingers . . .'

The artwork for the album also seems inspired by her role as Akasha. The cover is blood red, its tones repeated in an enticing inlay close-up of her pouting, slightly open mouth. In every picture she's draped in gold, most notably in the centre spread where her gold jewellery entwines itself serpent-like around her torso, almost bare except for a skimpy golden bikini top.

And yet she wasn't trying to play up to a bad girl role. As ever, the first in her list of 'thank-you's' was 'God, for his continued love and blessings,' while the album itself was dedicated to her beloved grandmother, Mintis, 'who, like the Sun, gave me sustenance and warmth, and, like the Moon, guided me through my darkest nights.' This was a young woman at ease with her sexuality, but not about to exploit it in a tawdry manner.

'The advantage is that being in this business you get to learn a lot, experience a lot of new things.'

'We Need a Resolution' itself is an inherently adult lyric, although not in an overtly sexual way. It's about a collapsing relationship, and the need for communication. There's no room for the wide-eyed idealism or slushy romanticism of Aaliyah's first two albums. The song portrays a woman in torment, confronting a man she suspects is two-timing her. But she doesn't bawl him out – she just asks him,'I want to know: Where'd you go instead?' Timbaland, playing the role of the bad guy, dismisses her with, 'I think I'm gonna get me a drink. I'll call you tomorrow.'

Not the most promising basis for a relationship.

The music continues the Middle Eastern musical theme that Aaliyah and Timbaland introduced on 'Try Again', a style that now seems redolent of her role as the Egyptian vampire queen in *Queen of the Damned*. They were pushing back the boundaries of R&B/hip-hop, digging the music out of its formulaic rut. Timbaland was now so confident of his musical experimentation that he even dispensed entirely with that mainstay of popular music, the bassline. When it was released as a single, Alex Needham described it in the *NME* as creating 'a universe of drama, suspicion and pain out of almost nothing. In other words, it's magic.'

Despite Timbaland's influence on Aaliyah's music, he only received a production credit for four tracks on the album (and one of those was for 'Try Again', borrowed from the *Romeo Must Die* soundtrack). Free rein was also given to other young bloods at the recording console, like Rapture and E. Seats, Bud'da, and J. Dub, a.k.a. Rockstar.

'Loose Rap' shows off the talents of another member of the Blackground family, Static from the Playa collective. Featuring an insidious, skeletal riff, echoing backing vocals and synthesised strings, it was Aaliyah's most hip-hop inflected track to date, dissing the smooth-talking, testosterone-packed players who would do her down if she let them. As she said of the track, 'It ain't just rhythm and blues.'

At first listen, 'Rock the Boat' sounds like a stylistic step backwards. It's a mid-tempo R&B song, with ghostly vocals and Eighties-style synths. Even the title was borrowed from

Biker chic; Aaliyah poses for Details *magazine, April 2000.*

a 1974 hit by the Hues Corporation. But take in the lyrics: with her calls to 'change positions', 'stroke it for me' and 'explore my body', the adult, all-woman Aaliyah was taking control. Rarely has an intense song about sexual satisfaction been delivered with such taste and elegance.

'More than a Woman' shares a title with another disco-era favourite, Tavares' 1978 classic. Timbaland is back in control here, demonstrating his trademark penchant for imaginative rhythms with an insistent motif

'I want people to look at me as a full on entertainer and a good person.'

on a guiro – a Brazilian percussion instrument that's scraped, rather than hit or shaken. Lyrically, it follows on seamlessly from the previous track: 'Midnight grindin', my heart rate's climbin'.'

But it wasn't just good loving in the world of Aaliyah. 'Never No More' is a heart-wrenching ballad that echoes some of the greatest soul singers of the Sixties. It deals with a difficult subject – physical abuse within a relationship – in a sensitive, rather than strident, manner. The narrator is torn between her love for the abuser and her disgust at what he's done, but she's decided on one thing: 'I just know you better not touch me again, or I'll walk away. / That is one game I refuse to play.' The song meant a great deal to Aaliyah, who described it as 'one of my favourites because of the subject matter. I'm proud of that song. I'm hoping a lot of women feel it.'

After all that fucking and fighting, 'I Care 4 U' is a gentle relief. Missy Elliott's sole lyric on the album is a departure for the usually in-ya-face Miss Demeanour, a sweet tale of a woman singling out a man who's been dumped. There's an immediate attraction, but she doesn't want to leap into bed with him – she just wants to talk, to let him know that somebody cares.

'I've never really had a boyfriend, and I don't have one now.'

'Extra Smooth' is musically unlike anything Aaliyah had tried before. The backing music, with its oompah bass, echoes the musical theatre of Brecht and Weill's *The Threepenny Opera* or Ebb and Kander's *Cabaret*. It's a comic putdown of a short-ass player who thinks he's bigger and smoother than he is. 'Get the boot,' sighs Aaliyah. His games just won't play with this lady.

'Read Between the Lines' is another snapshot of a relationship gone haywire. Staccato mariachi horns, clicky percussion and distorted vocals create an image of a loving woman in turmoil. 'I used to please him,' she sobs. 'U Got Nerve', which follows, could be the same couple's confrontation on the following day. Stripped-down electro pulses provide the backing to a woman striking out on her own, claiming, 'No longer am I a slave over your madness. / I am glad it's finally over.'

'I Refuse' delivers the same message in a completely different setting. A soft piano backing slowly builds into a massive, almost hymn-like arrangement. Static's lyric – 'I felt like I would die, if I could break down and cry / and I refuse to let you walk back through that door' – is shamelessly adapted from Gloria Gaynor's 1979 karaoke anthem, 'I Will

Aaliyah, at ease with the camera, at the MTV Movie Awards, June 2000.

Survive'. But Rockstar's production, encompassing everything from storm effects to Spanish guitar, at least matches the imaginative techniques of Timbaland.

'It's Whatever' reminds us that Aaliyah can do happy, as well as tortured. Superficially a gentle, summery love song, the groin-grinding woman is briefly let out of her box – 'so quit your stallin', my body's callin',' purrs the tigress.

'I Can Be' presents the flip-side of all those my-man-done-me-wrong lyrics, reminding us that Aaliyah the actress can switch roles. This time, she's 'another woman in your life', the other woman in a love triangle. (Whatever happened to the sisterly solidarity of 'If Your Girl Only Knew'?) Maybe a little of Queen Akasha's predatory sexuality had rubbed off on Baby Girl – the track was recorded in Melbourne while Aaliyah was doing her vampire thang. The *Queen of the Damned* soundtrack also exerts an influence, with feedback-drenched industrial synths and rock guitars making Aaliyah's sexual overtones sound as threatening as they are enticing.

'I have to honestly say that everything is worth it. The hard work, he times when you're tired, the times when you're sad.'

'Those Were the Days' is another break-up song, but it's laced with regret and nostalgia, rather than bile and vengeance. There's no reason for the split this time – simply, 'You don't please me no more.' Aaliyah sings the lyric coolly, almost robotically, over a bass and strings backing that harks back to the 1970s blaxploitation soundtracks of Isaac Hayes and Curtis Mayfield. It's only when she lapses into nostalgia for the times when the young lovers were just 'walking in the park' that she allows emotion to break in.

The other track from the Melbourne sessions is 'What If', which, like 'I Can Be', demonstrates Aaliyah's newfound passion for rockin' out. Snarling, Van Halen-esque guitar heroics are offset by industrial growls and synth stabs that hint at mid-period Duran Duran. Unfortunately, Rockstar, as a producer, gets so carried away with the instrumental embellishments that Aaliyah gets a little lost. Which is a pity, because the lyrics are among the best on the album, a witty, feminine rant that shows up the double standards of a man who's happy to flirt with every girl in town, but sees red when 'his' girl does the same thing.

The album closes with a reprise of 'Try Again', from *Romeo Must Die*. It serves as a reminder of her musical development over the space of a few short years. She was following her dream of being an all-round entertainer, but music was still her top priority. In the field of R&B, she was proving herself to be a genuine innovator.

Rolling Stone, which had been a little snobbish about Aaliyah's brand of studio-based, commercial R&B up till now, gave the album a coveted four-star rating. Their reviewer, Ernest Hardy, called *Aaliyah* 'a near-flawless declaration of strength and independence', on a par with Missy Elliott's *So Addictive* and Outkast's *Stankonia*. 'She's at the wheel, steering her sexuality and using it to explore her own fantasies and strength.' VH1.com labelled the crazed collision of sounds and influences as 'jukebox fare at a sci-fi cantina',

An ice (but nice) queen, Aaliyah poses for Details *magazine, April 2000.*

'*Keep working hard and you can
get anything you want.*'

and dubbed Aaliyah 'the shining light' of the new crop of female R&B performers.

John Mulvey in the *NME* highlighted 'the subtlety of it all, the tastefulness, the lack of bombast and histrionics . . . a gentle subversion of diva-dom.' He also observed how sane and reasonable Aaliyah sounded, in a universe still tainted by the East Coast/West Coast hip-hop wars that claimed Tupac, Biggie, and other, less famous figures: 'The vengeance fantasies and bling-bling lifestyles of so many of her contemporaries evidently hold little appeal for Aaliyah.' For it was simply not in Aaliyah's nature to live life with anything other than discipline and grace. As her fame soared her feet stayed firmly on the ground. Her publicist noted, 'She never takes a star trip. She's an angel', while Aaliyah herself insisted, 'I don't ever want to be one of those demanding divas. I was nice when I started out and I'm still nice now.' In the entertainment business, success often goes hand in hand with excess, sometimes with fatal consequences. But Aaliyah did not court danger of any kind, which makes it all the more painful that death claimed her at such a young age. Her work, along with her family, was something that kept her grounded, and allowed her scope for development. As she put it, 'I vow never to forget where I came from. I think it's important for people who listen to your music to feel they could BE you, that you're not this untouchable being.'

'I feel my image and signature style is unique and I never want to be afraid of trying different things.'

As a result of this approach, Aaliyah had been able to create an album that was suffused with sex and emotion, and resonated with her audience. All her experiences in the studio and in the outside world came together on Aaliyah. 'I'm a young adult now and this reflects my growth. It's about relationships – good ones, bad ones, even abusive ones,' she told an interviewer.

The album was Aaliyah's calling card, and this made it a huge success. Sales patterns for *Aaliyah* followed those of *One in a Million*. The singles struggled, none of them making the *Billboard* top twenty; but the album itself went roaring off the shelves. But while the lyrics to the songs on *Aaliyah* carried more than their share of heartache and pain, Aaliyah's own love life was finally granting her a degree of happiness.

After the negative publicity that followed her entanglement with R. Kelly, she seemed to have thrown herself into her work. But Aaliyah never gave away details of her private life in interviews,

'I wanted to be different and original but still have it be something the fans could get into.'

and this wasn't about to change. 'I've never really had a boyfriend, and I don't have one now,' she claimed. 'But when I do, I will try my best to keep what we do just for us.' Nevertheless, industry observers noted that a young man named Damon Dash was spending a lot of time in the company of Ms Haughton.

Aaliyah and Damon Dash, at the premiere of The Others, *Paris Theatre, New York, August 2001.*

Dash was the Chief Executive Officer of Roc-a-Fella records, the hip-hop label he launched with rap superstar Jay-Z in 1995. Still under 30, he'd signed a lucrative distribution deal with pioneering rap label Def Jam, and had also diversified into the fashion industry with the Roc-a-Fella clothing line.

> '*Damon and I are very good friends. I'll keep it at that right now.*'

Biased observers might have assumed Aaliyah's attraction to unsuitable men had struck again. For Dash was a product of Harlem's mean streets, who'd become involved with bad company when he lost his mother in his teens. He got back on track when he realised that material wealth could be found legitimately, by investing in musical talent. But he still had the brash attitude and foul mouth of his streetwise upbringing, and had managed to father two children on the road to success.

Aaliyah and Damon were beyond caring. She was no longer an innocent, romantically inclined kid, deluded by the smooth-talking of an R. Kelly. Aaliyah was in charge of her own career, and was going to see whoever she wanted to see. She had moved away from her parents' home in Detroit, and returned to New York, the city of her birth. She bought an apartment overlooking Central Park, and was relishing life in the city that never sleeps.

'I love it!' she said at the time. 'New York has its own energy. Sure, people come up to me in the street and say that they admire my work or whatever. I love being in the heart of it all – to be able to walk out of my apartment and go get a bagel or go shopping . . . This is home to me. I was born here and have a lot of friends here . . . I'm a New York kinda girl.' It was a blissful time, as Damon remembers: 'She was always down-to-earth. We'd pop into Macdonalds and people wouldn't believe it. Whether we were going to a store, a movie or just sitting at home, it was like our own private little party in our own little world.'

Not that she had much chance to relax. In June and July of 2001, Aaliyah recorded a video diary for MTV, largely shot in Paris, detailing the promotional work she was doing for her new album. It acknowledged both the fun that her career gave her, and the hard work required in order to achieve and maintain success: 'I have to honestly say that everything is worth it. The hard work, the times when you're tired, the times when you're a bit sad . . . I've got a career that's blossoming and still growing and I am truly blessed and I thank God for his blessings every chance that I get.'

And there was always time for fun. In one touching sequence in the video, Aaliyah and her pals are goofing around in an amusement park. Aaliyah is the bravest of them, eager to take the most hair-raising rides, sneering at a thrill-seeker who lost his lunch on the pavement. She's with her favourite hairstylist, 29-year-old Eric Foreman, a key member of her travelling entourage. But even Foreman, known as a joker, loses his smile as Aaliyah bullies him into joining her on a ride that catapults the two of them into the heavens.

After they come down, Foreman is grim-faced and unsteady, but Aaliyah seems buoyed up by the whole experience. The following day, as they watch the hilarious tape of Foreman's discomfort, Aaliyah says, wistfully, 'That's a memory I have forever.'

A little over a month later, both Aaliyah and Foreman would be dead.

Aaliyah and Damon Dash in a guarded pose at the premiere of Planet of the Apes, *August 2001.*

6: NEVER NO MORE

'I'm just beginning to show you what I'm made of.'

Aaliyah in her MTV diary, 2001

WITH THE SUCCESS OF HER THIRD ALBUM, Aaliyah's career had moved up another level. She wasn't just a big hitter in the fields of soul and R&B any more – she had the whole entertainment world at her feet. Her good looks and mysterious persona were a major draw on MTV, but sex appeal alone doesn't guarantee a great promo. For 'Rock the Boat', Blackground hooked her up with top-flight director Hype Williams, famed for his tongue-in-cheek confections for Puff Daddy, Missy Elliott, and others.

Another way to improve your chances of rotation on MTV is a lush location. So, it was no surprise that Aaliyah found herself on Abaco, one of the 700 Caribbean islands

'It's hard to say what I want my legacy to be, you know what I want people to say when I'm long gone.'

that form the Bahamas, in late August 2001. The archipelago of the Bahamas forms an arc of about 750 miles along the northern edge of the Caribbean Sea. Its semi-tropical climate and sublime beaches pull in over a million tourists every year – more than four times the permanent population of the islands themselves.

Filming on location seems glamorous and exciting, but, like so many aspects of the entertainment world, can be dull, repetitive, hard work. Ironically, shooting in a beautiful location can actually make things worse – there are enticing beaches and pure blue ocean in all directions, but the performer may have to mime a single line of a song 43 times, instead of chilling out in the sun. Still, Aaliyah was the consummate professional, never acting like a prima donna or throwing hissy fits. To Aaliyah this was all part of the job she had been born to do. She once described her existence thus: 'It is a glamorous life. Going to award shows, meeting people that you've admired, getting to dress up, it's fun. But there's a business side as well. When you're tired, you may not feel like doing an interview. You have to get up in the morning to take a flight that takes you overseas for 12 hours. Some of can be grueling. But it's work. And if you love it you love all of it. And I really do.'

After Hype Williams called 'Cut!' for the last time, Aaliyah said her goodbyes and made her way back to her private jet, with her entourage. She was keen to get back to New York City, to hook up again with her boyfriend, Damon Dash, and to prepare for her forthcoming appearance at the MTV Awards. Always keen to mix business with pleasure, she was accompanied by her hairstylist from the European tour. Eric Foreman – the campy goofball who didn't want to go on the amusement park ride – had no qualms about joining her on the twin-engined Cessna 402B aeroplane on runway 27 of Marsh Harbour airport, scheduled to make the 200-mile trip to Florida.

What happened next is open to conjecture. Some sources say the pilot, Luis Morales, told his passengers that they were carrying too much luggage. If this is the case, he seems to have lost the argument, as all nine of them boarded with all their belongings intact. The plane took off shortly after 6 p.m., and reached a height of about 80 feet. Then it suddenly banked to the left and nosedived into the swamps just beyond Marsh Harbour, where it burst into flames.

Seven people, including Aaliyah and Morales, died instantly. The only person still conscious was Aaliyah's 300-pound bodyguard, Scott Gallin, who repeatedly asked after his employer's welfare. He and the other two survivors would also succumb to their injuries over the next few hours.

The terrible news soon made its way around the world. The initial reaction was disbelief. Jermaine Dupri, who had worked with Aaliyah on *One in a Million*, was working in the studio at the time. He initially dismissed the news as a sick hoax, until it finally sank in that it was the cold, hard truth. His tribute was that of one musician to another: 'She took chances on her music. Just the softness of how she sang over them hard-ass beats, it was something different.'

'The reason she was a star to everybody is that she had her own identity. Nobody else sounded like Aaliyah.'

– Jermaine Dupri

Beyoncé Knowles of Destiny's Child, with whom Aaliyah had formed a friendship, was told the news as she left the stage in Indianapolis. She, and everyone around her, burst into tears. Later on, Beyonce lamented the loss of her friend. 'She was so sweet, always. She was one of the most beautiful people on the inside as well as out.' Meanwhile bad-ass white rapper Eminem was about to make his entrance at the Reading Festival in England. Shedding his hate-filled, chainsaw-wielding persona for a moment, he asked the audience

A fan pays tribute to Aaliyah at the famous shrine on Sunset Boulevard which was created a few days after her death.

'Her star had just begun to shine so brightly . . . I love Aaliyah, and I will miss her for the rest of my life.'
~ Gladys Knight

The white horse-drawn cart carrying Aaliyah leads the funeral procession up Park Avenue, where fans lined the streets to pay their respects.

'She was like blood, and I lost blood.'
~ Timbaland

White doves, symbols of peace, are released before the the assembled funeral guests, Mike Tyson seen in the foreground.

for a short period of silence.

In the months that followed, accident investigators discovered that the plane was indeed overloaded with luggage. But then it came to light that, only twelve days before the flight, Luis Morales had been put on probation for possession of crack cocaine, a fact that, under Federal Aviation Authority rules, should have made him ineligible to fly. Accusation and counter-accusation rang out. Aaliyah's parents – and the families of Eric Foreman and his assistant Anthony Dodd, who also died – filed lawsuits for negligence against Virgin Records, with whom Blackground had a licensing deal and who had chartered the plane for the video shoot. Allegations that Morales was not even qualified to pilot the plane put the spotlight on the

'She was exquisitely beautiful and full of light and love. As an artist she was only getting better.'
~ Michael Rymer

Bahamas-based Blackhawk Aviation, owners of the Cessna. Eventually, in July 2002, a coroner's report disclosed traces of cocaine and alcohol in Morales' system. Investigators also found traces of corrosion in the plane's fuel tank.

But Aaliyah's admirers were not concerned with the legal minutiae. Their Baby Girl was no more, a shining light snuffed out prematurely. Whether it was a case of pilot error, or one suitcase too many, seemed totally irrelevant. The sense of unfulfilled potential, that they would never know how high she might have climbed, was hard to bear. Bill Carpenter, who had previously worked as her publicist at Blackground, declared, 'black entertainment has lost the woman who would eventually have become the Diana Ross or Whitney Houston of the twenty-something generation.' British music critic Neil McCormick praised her abilities in every field, calling her 'a superstar in the making, the very model of a 21st-century, multi-talented, multi-tasking, multi-media icon.'

Those who knew her best highlighted her personal qualities and unspoiled charm. Her aunt, Gladys Knight, said, 'Her star had just begun to shine so brightly. Though she was ours for only a short time, what a time it was. I love Aaliyah, and I will miss her for the rest of my life.'

'She was one of those individuals that would light up a room. She always greeted you with a smile.'
~ P. Diddy

Legendary producer Quincy Jones described her as 'one of the sweetest girls in the world', while DMX said she was a 'down-to-earth sister with enough energy to put anyone on a cloud'.

Friends, fans, and industry figures were all stunned by the loss. Established and upcoming artists were united in praise of Aaliyah. Producer Rodney Jerkins, described how, 'She grew like crazy from the time I worked with her to the stuff she's doing now. She was trying to find herself before. But by the third album, she was more of a performer, she

Busta Rhymes and Amanda Lewis grieve for Aaliyah.

became more of an artist.' And young soul singer Alicia Keys paid tribute Aaliyah in her own way. 'Aaliyah's death had such an impact on me because even though I never met her, I believe you can get an idea of the essence of a person's spirit through her music and image – and I felt that her spirit was so good.' Lisa 'Left-Eye' Lopes, the feistiest firebrand of the female trio TLC, shared the general sense of shock. 'That has got to be one of the scariest ways to die,' she said in an interview with dotmusic.com. 'She had such a promising career ahead of her.' A few months later, Lopes would lose her own life in a similarly pointless car accident, while vacationing in the Central American country of Honduras.

'One day we will be together again . . . we will always love you.'
~ Janet Jackson

Damon Dash, whose romance with the star had just come into bloom, lamented, 'Words can't describe how much I will miss her. She was my best friend and will remain in my heart forever.' But Timbaland, whose rising career was intertwined with Aaliyah's, put it most succinctly: 'She was like blood, and I lost blood.'

There's a common pattern when a star performer dies tragically or prematurely. The deaths of Elvis Presley and John Lennon saw their records leap to the top of the charts. Other stars, such as Otis Redding and Jimi Hendrix, had their biggest commercial successes after their deaths. There are a number of reasons for this. Committed fans want to demonstrate allegiance to their idol – it's almost as if, by propelling their music to the top of the charts, they are making them 'live' just that little bit longer. But more casual admirers suddenly become aware of the stature of the dead star, possibly because the news media accompanies bulletins about the demise with snippets of his or her music. Some psychologists have even described it as a form of transferred guilt: people feel bad because they weren't committed to the performer while he or she was alive, and now want to make amends.

Record companies are in a difficult position when a major artist dies. If they rush-release extra copies of the artist's CDs, they're seen to be cashing in on a tragedy. But if they treat it as business as usual, then they're disregarding the fan market and the

'She was a wonderful and talented artist who will be missed by everyone whose lives she touched.'
~ Jet Li

record-buying public en masse. Whatever the morality of it, sales of Aaliyah's self-titled album rocketed in the weeks following her death, pushing it from the lower reaches of the *Billboard* Top Twenty to the top of the chart. The CD had been shifting in respectable quantities, about 60,000 units a week, in North America – in the week following the plane crash, nearly a third of a million people bought a copy. There was a similar shift in the United Kingdom: only 22,000 copies had been sold before her death, rocketing to 89,000 in the days following that fateful event in the Bahamas. Music fans who had only been vaguely aware of Aaliyah were suddenly confronted by the gap she left on the musical landscape.

The funeral took place six days after the accident, on 31 August 2001. Aaliyah's body was brought back to New York, the city where she was born just over 22 years before. The funeral service, at St Ignatius Catholic Church on Manhattan's legendary Park Avenue, was a star-studded affair. People who had worked with Aaliyah, from Missy Elliott to Jet Li, were in attendance, as were the cream of the black showbusiness community: P. Diddy, Mike Tyson, Chris Rock, Busta Rhymes, Jay-Z, Usher, and Li'l Kim. The fans were also out in force, lining the streets to catch a glimpse of the white horse-drawn carriage that took Aaliyah to her final resting place.

'Words can't describe how much I will miss her. She was my best friend and will remain in my heart forever.' ~ Damon Dash

But, despite all the trappings of celebrity, it was still the funeral of a daughter and a sister. It was, naturally, Aaliyah's family for whom the grief was most intense, and whose tributes were most poignant. The most heart-rending moment came when the singer's mother, Diane, sang 'One in a Million' over the coffin, before breaking down in tears. Aaliyah's brother Rashad somehow managed to maintain his composure as he read a eulogy, although the pain was etched on his face. 'I can see you smiling through the sunshine,' he announced, before asking the congregation to remember the other victims of the crash.

He still managed to keep his composure a week later, at the MTV Music Video Awards. Aaliyah had been due to present an award, and her absence hung over the ceremony like a dark cloud. Her closest collaborators, Missy Elliott and Timbaland, joined Rashad on stage to pay a brief, dignified tribute to the tragic star. Their dignity contrasted sharply with the inane fluff that comprised the rest of the show. (Britney Spears wiggled suggestively around the stage, wielding a huge albino python. Aaliyah had performed a similar routine, with considerably more elegance, in the promo for 'We Need a Resolution'. A tribute, or a tasteless goof? You choose.)

Life, as the cliché, has it, goes on. Post-production work was still going on for *The Queen of the Damned*. It's normal practice to bring actors back after their scenes have been shot, to re-dub parts of their dialogue. In Aaliyah's case it was now impossible, so the producers had to find someone with a similar vocal tone. Their choice was unusual, but entirely appropriate. In a final gesture of affection, Rashad Haughton stepped up to the microphone to complete his beloved sister's final performance. With no dramatic training, it's a tribute to his commitment that, on release, the audience couldn't detect the difference.

Of course, there were still some who felt duty-bound to take pot-shots at Aaliyah, while the rain still fell on her freshly dug grave. One *New York Post* journalist, Rod Dreher, argued that the lavishness of her funeral was out of all proportion. 'A traffic-snarling cortege in honour of a pop singer most people have never heard of? Give us a break!' he barked. And there were rumours that the whole ceremony had been funded by Blackground and/or Virgin as part of a posthumous publicity drive. Certainly, it was in dubious taste to film the procession for a tribute video – but probably not as tasteless as the 'fans' who immediately rushed out the tape *Losing Aaliyah*, containing a badly-staged re-enactment of the Cessna 402B's last few minutes.

Obviously her sudden end was a big story. After all it contained many of the essential

Aaliyah with her friend and collaborator Ginuwine at the Hot '97 Fashion Show, New York, 1997.

elements that enthrall people - youth, beauty, fame, violence, death. But society has always sanctified dead icons, extending way back before the modern entertainment industry to the martyrs of the Christian church. We may argue long into the night over whether James Dean and Marilyn Monroe, Jim Morrison, Janis Joplin, and Kurt Cobain, or Tupac Shakur and Notorious B.I.G. would have been as influential if they'd lived out a natural lifespan. What is clear is that people need heroes. And what is certain is that the death of any young person, be they famous or unknown, renders them immortal to those who loved them.

'She was like one of my daughters. She was one of the sweetest girls in the world.' ~ Quincy Jones

When the raunchy 'Rock the Boat' was released as a single in 2002, the *NME*'s John Robinson even described Aaliyah as 'the Tupac of R&B'. But this misses the point. Tupac lived his life on a knife-edge, eulogising the thug life, joking about imminent death. (The fact that he was a nice, middle-class boy, hardly entered into it.) Aaliyah stayed away from the dark side of the industry, never claiming to be any kind of authentic bad girl – in fact, her songs often made fun of the bling-bling lifestyle. On the only occasion her image had become tarnished, by her marriage to R. Kelly, she could justifiably present herself as a wronged party.

'Aaliyah inspired me not only to continue being an artist but to be an individual.'

~ Alicia Keys

One of the saddest things about Aaliyah's untimely end is that she never got the chance to enjoy the benefits of what she'd achieved. As she said shortly before she died, 'I'm 22, I've been in this since I was fifteen. I'm basically a veteran and yet I still have many places to go. I'm still young. I have no regrets. My parents made sure that I was involved in not just the show side of it, but the business side. One day I can sit back and seriously enjoy the fruits of my labour.' But, of course, fate had other plans.

Aaliyah and video director Hype Williams in New York, 1997.

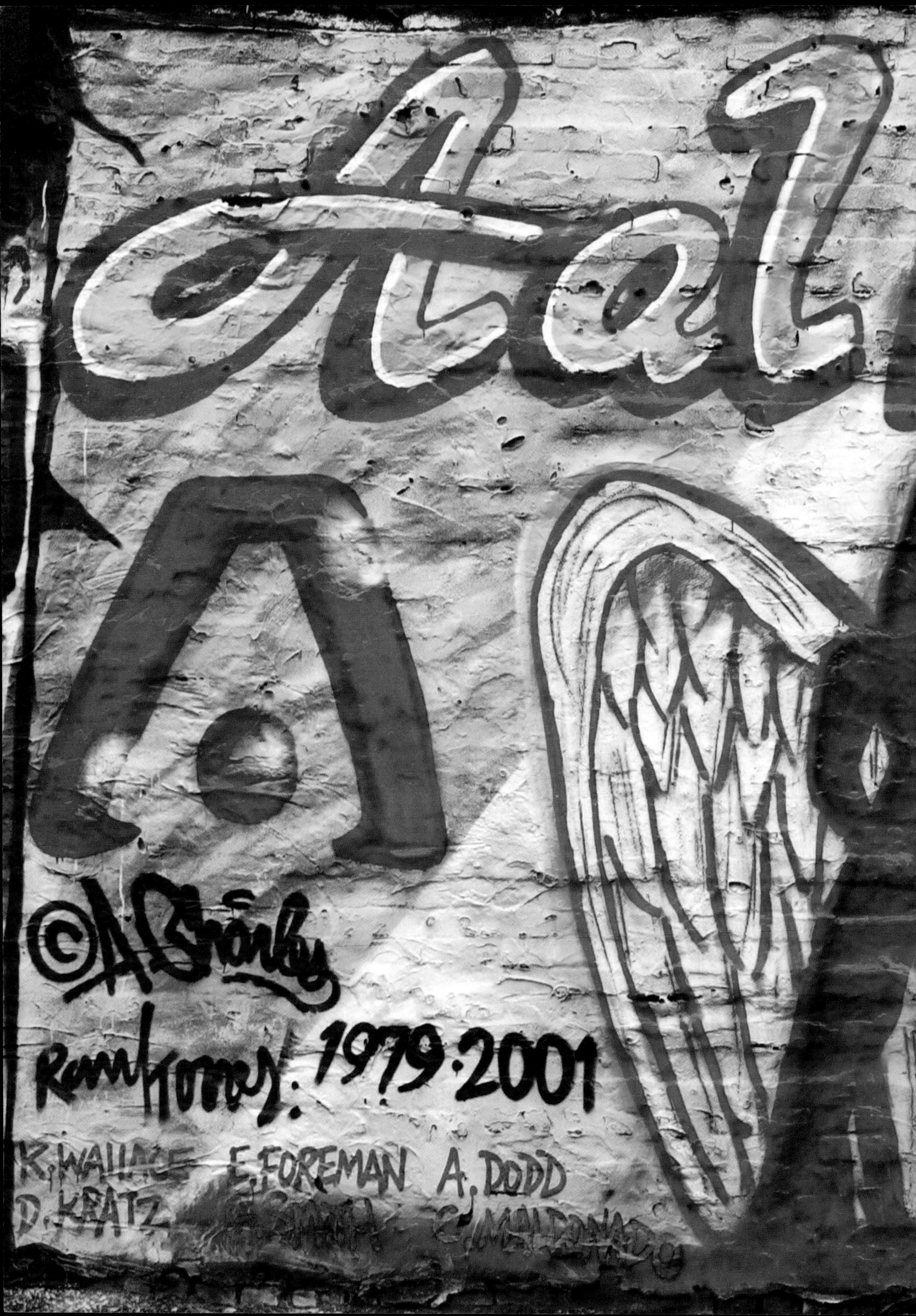
1979-2001
K. WALLACE
E. FOREMAN
A. DODD

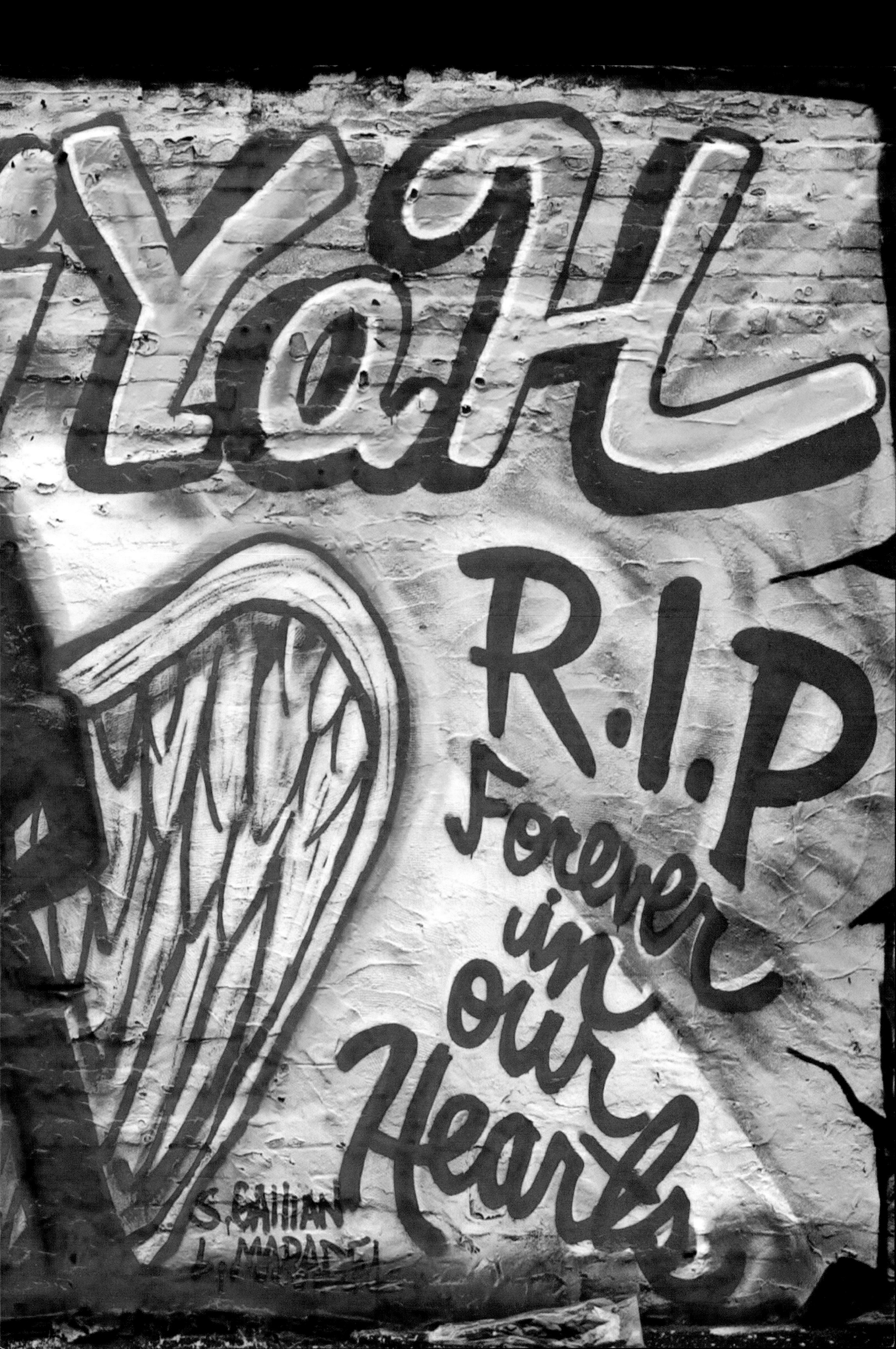
R.I.P
Forever in our Hearts

During Aaliyah's lifetime, when it came to awards it was a case of always the bridesmaid, never the bride – with the exception of a couple of MTV gongs. In the months following her death, she was posthumously awarded two prizes at the American Music Awards, while 'Rock the Boat' earned her a *Soul Train* Award for Best R&B/Soul Single, Female. Well into 2002, even approaching the first anniversary of her death, Aaliyah continued to earn nominations – including the *Billboard* R&B award, and the *Soul Train* Lady of Soul award. It took a dreadful tragedy to alert the entertainment industry to Aaliyah's unique talents.

Three albums, two movies, a handful of other recordings, and a few exceptional promo videos: pretty good for a lifespan of just 22 years. Aaliyah hardly ever appeared live on stage after accompanying Gladys Knight in Las Vegas, which puts her in the bad books of purists who like performers to pay their dues. She was always guarded in interviews, even to the extent of keeping her major romantic relationships – with R. Kelly and Damon Dash – as closely guarded secrets. Some claim this was all part of an attempt to give herself a mysterious allure. Vincent Jackson, a writer for the British dance music magazine *Mixmag*, described her as 'a minority pursuit', claiming 'in two years' time people will forget about her.'

'She was so sweet and so talented and it's just tragic.''
~ Beyonce Knowles

But these are the sentiments of hard-bitten hacks and jaded industry insiders. If you really want to assess the impact that Aaliyah made, look toward the fans. Think of the spontaneous tributes that sprang up as soon as the terrible news began filtering through from Abaco. Think of the massive advertising billboard for her final album on Sunset Boulevard, plastered with flowers and scrawled, tear-stained tributes. Think of the flowers, candles, teddy bears, and cards piled up around Cipriani's restaurant on New York's East 42nd Street, which, hired by Virgin Records for the occasion, became a shrine to Aaliyah. Think of the grief-filled messages that ricocheted

'I love you Aaliyah and you're forever missed.'
~ Missy Elliot

around the internet, the tribute sites constructed with more love than technical skill. Perhaps the most touching tribute, and the way she'll really be remembered, came in the months following the star's death. Until 2001, the name 'Aaliyah' was practically unknown outside the Muslim world. In early 2002, the US Department of Social Services reported that it was one of the top 100 most popular name for newborn girls in the United States.

Aaliyah's fans continue to feel that they have a special relationship with her. She did all her growing up in public – an ordinary kid from an ordinary family, but blessed with an extraordinary talent. As fourteen-year-old Holly Churney told *Rolling Stone*, as she joined the New York vigil: 'I liked her because she wasn't such a flashy artist. She let her music speak for her.'

Aaliyah would have been thrilled to hear this. She spoke often about her raison d'etre,

Previous page: A mural tribute to Aaliyah is painted on the side of a building on August 27, 2001 on the Lower East Side of New York City.

'the fact that you can touch someone so deeply by what you do. The fact that you can go overseas in Japan and Europe and have those people know every lyric to the point where some are bought to tears . . . there's no feeling like that. It's really beyond words. That's what makes everything worthwhile.'

'Aaliyah was my best friend . . . she was always an angel from the first day she was born.'
~ Rashad Haughton

Aaliyah did speak to us through her songs, and her work continues to move thousands worldwide.

We mourn Aaliyah.

At least we still have the music.

DISCOGRAPHY

ALBUMS

AGE AIN'T NOTHIN' BUT A NUMBER
(US: Blackground/Jive; UK: Jive; 1994)
Intro / Throw Your Hands Up / Back And
Forth / Age Ain't Nothing But A Number
/ Down With The Clique / At Your Best
(You Are Love) / No One Knows How To
Love Me Quite Like You Do / I'm So Into
You / Street Thing / Young Nation / Old
School / I'm Down / Back And Forth (Mr.
Lee and R. Kelly Mix)

ONE IN A MILLION (US: Blackground;
UK: Virgin; 1996)
Beats 4 Da Streets (Intro) / Hot Like Fire
/ One In A Million / A Girl Like You / If
Your Girl Only Knew / Choosey Lover
(Old School/New School) / Got To Give
It Up / 4 Page Letter / Everything's
Gonna Be Alright / Giving You More / I
Gotcha Back / Never Givin' Up /
Heartbroken / Never Comin' Back /

Ladies In Da House / The One I Gave My
Heart To / Came To Give Love (Outro)

AALIYAH (US: Blackground; UK:
Blackground/Virgin; 2001)
We Need A Resolution (featuring
Timbaland) / Loose Rap (featuring Static
from Playa) / Rock The Boat / More Than
A Woman / Never No More / I Care 4 U /
Extra Smooth / Read Between The Lines /
U Got Nerve / I Refuse / It's Whatever / I
Can Be / Those Were The Days /What If.
The special edition of the album contains a
bonus disc with video tracks: Aaliyah
Introduction / One In A Million / Are You
That Somebody? / Try Again / We Need A
Resolution / Aaliyah (Behind The Scenes).
The Australian edition (on EMI) contains
an extra track, Try Again (from the *Romeo
Must Die* soundtrack).

CONTRIBUTIONS TO SOUNDTRACK
ALBUMS

LOW DOWN DIRTY SHAME (US:
BMG/Jive/Silvertone; 1995)
The Thing I Like

SUNSET PARK (US: WEA/Elektra; 1996)
Are You Ready

SPRUNG (US: Warner Brothers; 1997)
One In A Million (remix)

*ANASTASIA: MUSIC FROM THE MOTION
PICTURE* (US: Atlantic; UK: Warner
Brothers; 1997)
Journey To The Past

DR DOOLITTLE (US: Atlantic; UK:
Warner Brothers; 1998)
Are You That Somebody?

MUSIC OF THE HEART (US/UK: Sony;
1999)
Turn The Page

ROMEO MUST DIE: THE ALBUM
(US/UK: Virgin, 2000)
Try Again / Come Back In One Piece /
Are You Feelin' Me? / I Don't Wanna

NEXT FRIDAY (US: Priority; 2000)
I Don't Wanna
(The album is available in 'clean' and
'explicit' versions)

*COMPILATION ALBUM TRACKS VOL. 1 –
SMOOTH LOVE JAMS* (US: Beast; 1997)
At Your Best You Are Love

ALL THAT (US: Loud; 1999)
Age Ain't Nothing But A Number

NOW THAT'S WHAT I CALL MUSIC! 4
(US: Polygram; 2000)
Try Again

NOW THAT'S WHAT I CALL MUSIC! 8
(US: Polygram; 2001)
Rock The Boat

NOW THAT'S WHAT I CALL MUSIC! 10
(US: Polygram; 2002)
More Than A Woman

*VARIOUS ARTISTS: A TRIBUTE TO
AALIYAH* (US: Big Eye Music; 2002)
Back And Forth / At Your Best You Are
Love / Age Ain't Nothing But A Number /
Got To Give It Up / The One I Gave My
Heart To / Journey To The Past / Are You
That Somebody? / Try Again / I Don't
Wanna / We Need A Resolution / More
Than A Woman / I Care 4 U.
(This tribute album by anonymous R&B
performers was a fundraiser for breast can-
cer awareness. It was a cause particularly
close to Aaliyah's heart after she lost her
grandmother to the disease.)

SINGLES
Back And Forth (LP version) / Back And
Forth (Mr. Lee and R. Kelly's remix)
(Blackground/Jive; 1994)
At Your Best You Are Love
(Blackground/Jive; 1994)
Age Ain't Nothing But A Number
(Blackground/Jive; 1995)
Down with the Clique (Blackground/Jive;
1995)
The Thing I Like (Blackground/Jive;
1995)
Got To Give It Up (Atlantic; 1996)
I Need You Tonight (with Junior MAFIA)
(Atlantic; 1996)
If Your Girl Only Knew (Atlantic; 1997)
4 Page Letter (Atlantic; 1997)
The One I Gave My Heart To (Atlantic;
1997)
The One I Gave My Heart To '98: The
One I Gave My Heart To (Soul Solution
club mix) / The One I Gave My Heart To
(Soul Solution dub) / One In A Million
(Nitebreed Mongolidic mix) / One In A

Million (Geoffrey's house mix) / One In
A Million (Armand's drum 'n' bass mix) /
One In A Million (Wolf D big bass mix) /
One In A Million (Nitebreed dub)
Journey To The Past (Atlantic; 1998)
Are You That Somebody? (Atlantic; 1998)
Try Again (album version) / Try Again
(Timbaland remix) / Try Again (D'Jam
Hassan remix) / Try Again (instrumental)
(Blackground/Virgin; 2000)
I Don't Wanna / Come Back In One Piece
(with DMX) (Blackground/Virgin, 2000)
We Need A Resolution / Messed Up / Are
You Feelin' Me? / We Need A Resolution
(video) (Blackground/Virgin, 2001)
More Than A Woman / More Than A
Woman (Bump & Flex club mix) / More
Than A Woman (MAW main mix)
(Blackground/Virgin, 2002)
Rock The Boat / Rock The Boat (club mix
by Mixzo) / Rock The Boat (club mix by
Doug Lazy) (Blackground/Virgin; 2002)

ACKNOWLEDGEMENTS

We would like to thank the following authors, journalists, newspapers, and magazines whose books, interviews and articles on Aaliyah were invaluable:

Aaliyah: More Than A Woman, by Christopher John Farley, (MTV Books/Pocket Books 2001); 'Death Becomes Her' by Fiona Sturgess, *Life Etc*, (*The Independent on Sunday*) 10 February 2002; 'Dead Famous' by Lori Majewski, *The Sunday Times Magazine* (*The Sunday Times*), August 25 2002; 'The Lady Is A Vamp', by Glenn Waldrom, *i-D*, September 2001; 'Aaliyah: R&B Star Too Young To Die' by Michael Hogan, *Marie-Claire* 2003; 'A Damned Production' by Debra Campbell, *Bite Me,* Issue 8, Spring 2001.

We would like to thank the following websites, magazines, and newspapers for their coverage of Aaliyah, in particular: Aaliyah.com, Aaliyah2001.com, Aaliyahonline.com, Aaliyahtellya2.republika.pl, Angelfire.com, Diana-drubig.de, Its_all_bout_howie.tripod.com; *Billboard, Blackbeat, Blaze, Blender, Daily Telegraph, Dallas Morning News, Details, Empire, Entertainment Weekly, EW, Fashion Wire Daily, Hollywood Reporter, Honey, Metro, Movieline, NME, People, Pride, Q, Rap Pages, Right On!, Seventeen, Teen, Teen People, The Evening Standard, The Guardian, The Independent, The Source, The Times, Time Magazine, Total Film, TV Hits, USA Today, Vanity Fair, Variety, Vibe, XXL, YM,* www.bbc.co.uk, musicgala.com, www.mtv.com, www.nme.com, Q4Music.com, www.rollingstone.com, soultrain.com.

We would like to thank the following photographers, photographic agencies, film companies and libraries: Marc Baptiste/Corbis Outline; Barron Claiborne/Corbis Outline; Christopher Kolk/Corbis Outline; Eric Johnson/Corbis Outline; George Lange/Corbis Outline; Dana Lixenburg/Corbis Outline; Carl Posey/Corbis Outline; Ezio Petersen/Corbis Sygma; Frank Trapper/Corbis Sygma; Pauline French/Famous; Dimitrious Kambouris/Retna Ltd; Frederick M Brown/Getty Images; Patrick McMullan/Getty Images; Spencer Platt/Getty Images; Movie Market; Fitzroy Barrett/Retna Ltd USA; Michael Benanbib/Retna Ltd USA; Monique Bunn/Retna Ltd USA; Larry Busacca/Retna Ltd USA; Steve Granitz/Retna Ltd USA; Joseph Marzullo/Retna Ltd USA; Ernie Paniccioli/Retna Ltd; Kelly A. Swift/Retna Ltd USA, Warner Bros.

It has not been possible in all cases to trace the copyright sources, and the publishers would be glad to hear from any such unacknowledged copyright holders.